WORLD-CLASS WAREHOUSING AND MATERIAL HANDLING

WORLD-CLASS WAREHOUSING AND MATERIAL HANDLING

Edward Frazelle

McGraw-Hill
New York   Chicago   San Francisco   Lisbon   London
Madrid   Mexico City   Milan   New Delhi   San Juan
Seoul   Singapore   Sydney   Toronto

Library of Congress Cataloging-in-Publication Data

Frazelle, Edward.
    World-class warehousing and material handling / by Edward Frazelle.
        p.   cm
    Includes bibliographical references.
    ISBN 0-07-137600-3
    1. Warehouses—Management   2. Materials handling.   I. Title.

HF5485 F69 2001
658.7'85—dc21   2001045281

McGraw-Hill

A Division of The McGraw·Hill Companies

6 7 8 9 0   DOC/DOC   0 7 6

ISBN 0-07-137600-3

The sponsoring editor for this book was Catherine Dassopoulos. It was set in Times New Roman by MacAllister Publishing Services, LLC.

Printed and bound by R.R. Donnelley & Sons Company.

This book is dedicated to my Lord Jesus Christ, my wife Pat, and my children Kelly and Andrew.

Contents

WORLD-CLASS WAREHOUSING AND MATERIAL HANDLING

1

INTRODUCTION: WHY HAVE A WAREHOUSE?

WITH SO MANY ATTEMPTS to eliminate inventory and warehousing in the supply chain, why should you read a book on warehousing?

1.1 SUPPLY CHAIN IMBALANCES

Despite all of the initiatives in e-commerce, supply chain integration, efficient consumer response, quick response, and just-in-time delivery, the supply chain connecting manufacturing with end consumers will never be so well coordinated that warehousing will be completely eliminated. However, as these initiatives take hold, the role and mission of warehouse operations are changing and will continue to change dramatically. This book holds up flexibility as the key to success in warehousing and describes how to increase the flexibility of warehouse operations through process design, system selection and justification, and layout configuration.

1.2 HIGH-SPEED, ZERO DEFECT SUPPLY CHAINS

Supply chain integration initiatives to minimize pipeline inventory severely reduce the margin for error in supply chain logistics. Hence, the accuracy and cycle time performance pressures in warehousing are immense. This books defines world-class accuracy and cycle time performance goals and defines the world-class processes that yield world-class accuracy and cycle time.

1.3 VALUE-ADDED WAREHOUSING

Warehouses play vital roles in the supply chain (see Figure 1-1).

Raw material and component warehouses   Hold raw materials at or near the point of induction into a manufacturing or assembly process.

Work-in-process warehouses   Hold partially completed assemblies and products at various points along an assembly or production line.

Finished goods warehouses   Hold inventory used to balance and *buffer* the variation between production schedules and demand. For this purpose, the warehouse is usually located near the point of manufacture and is often characterized by the flow of full pallets in and full pallets out, assuming that product size and volume warrant pallet-sized loads. A warehouse serving only this function may have demands ranging from monthly to quarterly replenishment of stock to the next level of distribution.

FIGURE 1-1   The roles of a warehouse in logistics and supply chain management.

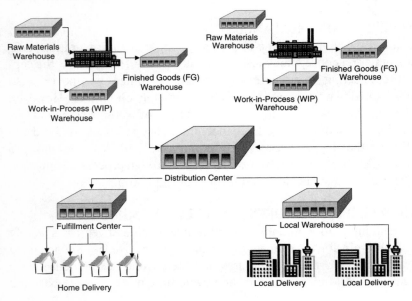

Distribution warehouses and distribution centers   Accumulate and consolidate products from various points of manufacture within a single firm, or from several firms, for combined shipment to common customers. Such a warehouse may be located central to either the production locations or the customer base. Product movement may be typified by full pallets or cases in and full cases or broken case quantities out. The facility is typically responding to regular weekly or monthly orders.

Fulfillment warehouses and fulfillment centers   Receive, pick, and ship small orders for individual consumers.

Local warehouses   Distributed in the field in order to shorten transportation distances to permit *rapid response* to customer demand. Frequently, single items are picked, and the same item may be shipped to the customer every day.

Value-added service warehouses   Serve as the facility where key product customization activities are executed, including packaging, labeling, marking, pricing, and returns processing.

This book describes the processes and systems required for the warehouse to satisfy each of these mission statements.

Figure 1-1 illustrates warehouses performing these functions in a logistics network. Unfortunately, in many of today's networks, a single item will pass in and out of warehouses serving each of these functions between the point of manufacture and the customer. When feasible, two or more missions should be combined in the same warehousing operation, and handling steps in the chain should be minimized. Current changes in the availability and cost of transportation options make combining activities in a single location and link skipping possible for many products. In particular, small high-value items with unpredictable demand are frequently shipped worldwide from a single source using overnight delivery services.

1.4   RISING WAREHOUSING COSTS

Warehousing is expensive—making up between 2 and 5 percent of the cost of sales of a corporation. With renewed corporate emphasis on return-on-assets, minimizing the cost of warehousing has become an important business issue. At the same time, continued emphasis on customer service places most warehouse managers between a rock and a hard place—looking for ways to trim costs and improve customer service at the same time. This book is written with this challenge in mind and provides a variety of process improvement suggestions aimed at improving warehouse resource utilization while maintaining and/or improving customer service.

1.5   CONFUSION AND CROWDING IN THE WAREHOUSE MARKETPLACE

The warehousing marketplace is confused and crowded with hundreds of suppliers of warehouse management systems, hundreds of third-party warehousers, and hundreds of warehousing consultants. This book was written to make you a better consumer in the marketplace, equipping you to separate the wheat from the tares.

1.6   THE PLIGHT OF THE WAREHOUSE MANAGER

Under the influence of e-commerce, supply chain collaboration, globalization, quick response, and just-in-time, warehouses today are being asked to

*   Execute *more*, smaller transactions
*   Handle and store *more* items
*   Provide *more* product and service customization
*   Offer *more* value-added services
*   Process *more* returns
*   Receive and ship *more* international orders

    At the same time, warehouses today have

*   *Less* time to process an order
*   *Less* margin for error
*   *Less* young, skilled, English-speaking personnel
*   *Less* WMS capability (a byproduct of Y2K investments in ERP systems)

    I call this "rock and a hard place" scenario the plight of the warehouse manager. Never has the warehouse been asked to do so much and at the same time been so strapped for resources.

1.7   LOGISTICS LITIGATION

One barometer we have for the focus of business on the warehouse is the number of requests for expert witness work we receive. In the last year, we have had an unprecedented number of requests for expert witness work related to failed warehouse management or material handling systems. The fault is about evenly divided between vendors and users; however, the number of calls is a testimony to the value that corporations are placing on warehouse operations. Never before has it been so critical for the warehouse to work efficiently, quickly, and error free.

The bottom line is that the warehouse is playing a more vital role in the success (or failure) of businesses today than it ever has. This book describes the principles of warehousing that yield world-class warehousing operations. The principles follow our warehouse master planning methodology (see Figure 1-2) and cover the following:

*   Investigating warehouse operations (Section I) through warehouse activity profiling (Chapter 2) and warehouse performance benchmarking (Chapter 3)
*   Innovating, optimizing, and simplifying warehouse operations (Section II) in receiving and put-away (Chapter 4), storage (Chapters 5-7), order picking (Chapter 8), shipping (Chapter 9), and material flow (Chapter 10)

FIGURE 1-2   Warehouse master planning methodology.

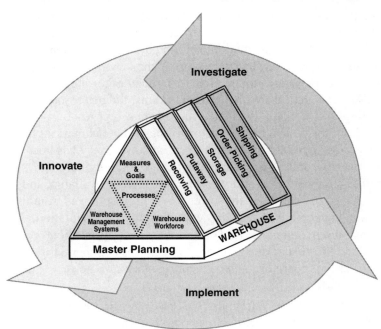

- Implementing new warehousing designs (Section III) in computerizing warehouse operations (Chapter 11), and humanizing warehouse operations (Chapter 12)

World-Class Warehousing presents an organized set of principles that separate world-class warehouse operations from middle- and no-class warehouse operations. The principles were developed during a retrospective review of hundreds of warehousing projects, including greenfield warehouse designs, warehouse layout designs, warehouse operations benchmarking, warehouse process improvement, and warehouse management systems design and implementation. These principles are the *common denominators* of the successful projects and successful warehouse operations. In order, they are

1. **Profile**   Create and maintain order profiles, item activity profiles, and planning profiles to identify root causes of process impediments and breakthrough opportunities for improvement.

2. **Benchmark**   Benchmark warehouse performance, practices, and operating infrastructure against world-class standards to determine performance, practice, and infrastructure gaps, to quantify opportunities for improvement, and to estimate the affordable investment in new material and information handling systems.

   Profiling (Chapter 2) and benchmarking (Chapter 3) amount to doing your homework before an exam. In this case, the exam is process redesign, material and information handling systems design, and systems implementation. The exam score is the new productivity, cycle time, accuracy, and storage density indicators for the warehouse. As is the case with academic exams, the better job you do in preparing for the exam, the better your exam score. Another way to think about this is that during the profiling and benchmarking process, no redesign has been set in stone, and no money has been spent on new systems. It is during this stage of a re-engineering project that the most opportunity for improvement is available, and the cost of design changes is the lowest. As a project moves from the preliminary concepting phase into detail design, implementation, debugging, and maintenance, the opportunity for improvement degrades and the cost of design changes increases exponentially. As a result, the early preparatory and concepting phases of a project are the most important.

3. **Innovate**   Reconfigure warehouse processes by eliminating and streamlining as much work content as possible. Because most of the

work in a warehouse is material and information handling, these two activities should be the focus of the process redesign initiatives.

Innovation (Chapters 4–10) follows profiling and benchmarking because the project team needs the warehouse activity profile to creatively generate new, minimum work content processes and needs the benchmarking results to know the performance goals of the new processes and to know how much capital is available for new systems.

4.   **Automate**   To automate means to *computerize* and to *mechanize*. *Computerizing* is to incrementally justify and incrementally implement warehouse management systems, paperless warehousing systems, and decision support tools to maintain the warehouse activity profile, to track warehouse performance and resource utilization, and to enforce simplified warehouse processes. *Mechanizing* is to incrementally justify and incrementally implement mechanized material handling and storage systems to improve warehouse throughput and storage density and to assist warehouse operators in difficult material handling activities.

Computerizing (Chapter 11) follows innovation because the primary role of the computer is to enforce and monitor the new, simple processes. The warehouse management systems and paperless warehousing system requirements should flow naturally from the process definitions developed during simplification.

Mechanization (taught throughout) follows computerizing because the simplification and computerizing process should minimize the amount of mechanization required. Investments in mechanized systems are inherently less flexible than investments in computer software and hardware.

5.   **Humanize**   Humanize warehouse operations by involving warehouse operators in redesigning warehouse processes, by developing team and individual performance goals, and by implementing ergonomic improvements in every manual activity in the warehouse.

Humanizing (Chapter 12) is the last of the seven steps, not because the operators are the least important resource in the warehouse (in fact, just the opposite is true), but because the full skill set and cultural requirements for the workforce are not known until each of the first principles have been applied. The only advice I can give in this area is very old advice—treat people the way you would like to be treated. It works every time.

Applied in this order, these principles can and have been used to create warehousing master plans, to reengineer warehousing operations, to guide warehouse process improvement projects, and to develop requirements for warehouse management systems. I hope you will find them useful in similar projects.

If you are already familiar with the field of warehousing, please move onto the first step: profiling. If you are new to the field, the following review of warehousing basics may be helpful.

1.8   WAREHOUSING FUNDAMENTALS

Though warehousing is increasing in importance in logistics and supply chain management, it is still integrated with and to a large degree dependent on other logistics activities. In fact, in our teaching and consulting, we present warehousing as the last of the five logistics activities (see Figure 1-3) for a variety of reasons. First, good planning in the other four areas of logistics may eliminate the need for warehousing. Second, requirements in the other four areas of logistics may suggest that a third-party warehousing firm should be retained to operate the warehouse. Third, the warehouse must be designed to meet all the requirements of the customer service policy spelled out in the customer response master plan, house all the inventory required by the inventory master plan, work to receive in quantities stipulated by the supply master plan, and serve a mission stipulated by the transportation master plan. The warehouse is a service to all the other areas of logistics.

Despite the name or role, warehouse operations have a fundamental set of activities in common. The following list includes the activities found in most warehouses. These tasks, or functions, are also indicated on a flow line in Figure 1-4 to make it easier to visualize them in actual operation.

1.   Receiving
2.   Prepackaging (optional)
3.   Putaway
4.   Storage
5.   Order picking
6.   Packaging and/or pricing (optional)
7.   Sortation and/or accumulation
8.   Unitizing and shipping

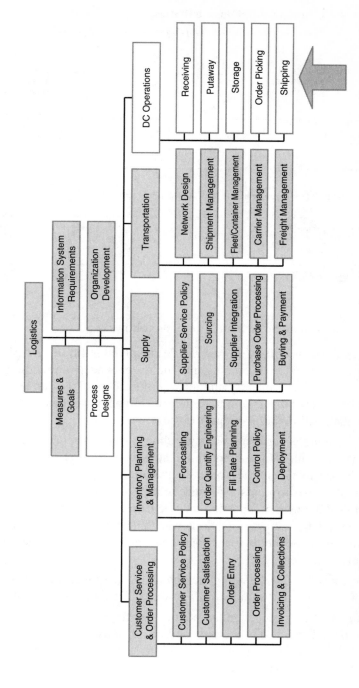

FIGURE 1-3 Warehousing in the logistics framework.

9

FIGURE 1-4   Common warehouse activities.

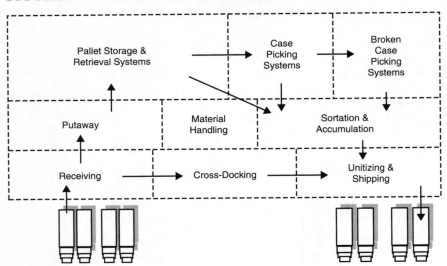

The functions may be defined briefly as follows:

1.   *Receiving* is the collection of activities involved in (a) the orderly receipt of all materials coming into the warehouse, (b) providing the assurance that the quantity and quality of such materials are as ordered, and (c) disbursing materials to storage or to other organizational functions requiring them.

2.   *Prepackaging* is performed in a warehouse when products are received in bulk from a supplier and subsequently packaged singly, in merchandisable quantities, or in combinations with other parts to form kits or assortments. An entire receipt of merchandise may be processed at once, or a portion may be held in bulk form to be processed later. This may be done when packaging greatly increases the storage-cube requirements or when a part is common to several kits or assortments.

3.   *Putaway* is the act of placing merchandise in storage. It includes material handling, location verification, and product placement.

4.   *Storage* is the physical containment of merchandise while it is awaiting a demand. The storage method depends on the size and quantity of the items in inventory and the handling characteristics of the product or its container.

5.   *Order picking* is the process of removing items from storage to meet a specific demand. It is the basic service a warehouse provides for customers and is the function around which most warehouse designs are based.

6.   *Packaging* and/or *pricing* may be done as an optional step after the picking process. As in the prepackaging function, individual items or assortments are containerized for more convenient use. Waiting until after picking to perform these functions has the advantage of providing more flexibility in the use of on-hand inventory. Individual items are available for use in any of the packaging configurations right up to the time of need. Pricing is current at the time of sale. Prepricing at manufacture or receipt into the warehouse inevitably leads to some repricing activity as price lists are changed while merchandise sits in inventory. Picking tickets and price stickers are sometimes combined into a single document.

7.   *Sortation* of batch picks into individual orders and *accumulation* of distributed picks into orders must be done when an order has more than one item and the accumulation is not done as the picks are made.

8.   *Unitizing* and *shipping* may include the following tasks:
   • Checking orders for completeness
   • Packaging merchandise in appropriate shipping containers
   • Preparing shipping documents, including packing lists, address labels and bills of lading
   • Weighing shipments to determine shipping charges
   • Accumulating orders by outbound carrier
   • Loading trucks (in many instances, this is a carrier's responsibility)

For discussion purposes, this book includes in *receiving* those activities described previously as receiving, prepackaging, and putaway; in *order picking*, those activities described previously as order picking, packaging, and sortation/accumulation; and in *shipping*, those activities described as unitizing and shipping.

S E C T I O N

I

INVESTIGATING WAREHOUSE OPERATIONS

C H A P T E R

2

WAREHOUSE ACTIVITY PROFILING: MINING FOR GOLD

S UPPOSE YOU WERE SICK and went to a doctor for a diagnosis and prescription. When you arrived at the doctor's office, he or she already had a prescription waiting for you, without even talking to you, let alone looking at you, examining you, doing blood work, and so on. In effect, he diagnosed you with his eyes closed and a random prescription generator. Needless to say, you would not be going back to that doctor for treatment.

Unfortunately, the prescriptions for many sick warehouses are written and implemented without much examination nor testing. For lack of knowledge, lack of tools, and/or lack of time, many warehouse reengineering and layout projects commence without any understanding of the root cause of the problems and without exploration of the real opportunities for improvement.

Warehouse activity profiling is the systematic analysis of item and order activity. The activity profiling process is designed to quickly identify root causes of material and information flow problems, to pinpoint major opportunities for process improvements, and to provide an objective basis for project-team decision making. We will start with some of the major motivations and potential roadblocks to successful profiling. Then we will review a full set of example profiles and their interpretations. The examples serve to teach the principles of profiling and as an outline for the full set of profiles required for reengineering your warehouse or distribution center. We will finish with the data gathering, data compilation, data analysis, and data presentation process required in profiling.

2.1 PROFILING MOTIVATIONS AND MINEFIELDS

Profiling Pays

Done properly, profiling quickly reveals warehouse design and planning opportunities that might not naturally be in front of you. Profiling quickly eliminates options that really aren't worth considering to begin with. Many warehouse re-engineering projects go awry because we work on a concept that never really had a chance in the first place. Profiling provides the right baseline to begin justifying new investments. Profiling gets key people involved. During the profiling process, it is natural to ask people from many affected groups to provide data, to verify and rationalize data, and to help interpret results. My partner Hugh Kinney says that, "People will only successfully implement what they design themselves." To the extent people have been involved, they feel that they have helped with the design process. Finally, profiling permits and motivates objective decision making as opposed to biased decisions made with little or no analysis or justification. I worked with one client whose team leader we affectionately called Captain Carousels. No matter what the data said, no matter what the order and profiles looked like, no matter what the company could afford, we were going to have carousels in the new design. You can imagine how successful that project was.

You can drown in a shallow lake — on average.

You will see a lot of complex statistical distributions in our journey through warehouse activity profiling. Why go to all the trouble?

Imagine we are trying to determine the average number of items on an order. Suppose we did the analysis based on a random sampling of 100 orders. In Figure 2-1, 50 orders are for one line, 0 are for two items, and 50 are for three items. What is the average number of items per order? It's two. How often does that happen? It never happens. If we are not careful to plan and design based on distributions as opposed to averages, the entire planning and design process will be flawed. That is why it is so important to go to the extra step to derive these profile distributions.

FIGURE 2-1   **Example items per order distribution.**

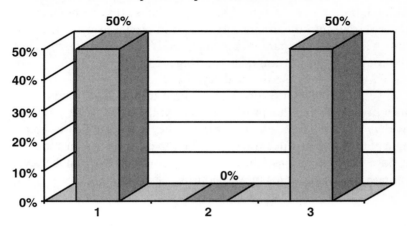

Wallowing in the Data Stimulates Creative Thinking

When I write a new article or book, one of the first things I do to stimulate my own thinking is to read what other people have written about the particular topic. If I am preparing to teach a Sunday school class or a seminar, I do the same thing. I review what other people have prepared on the topic to stimulate my thinking and to avoid reinventing the wheel. (You know the difference between plagiarism and research—plagiarism is when you borrow from a single author; research is when you borrow from many.)

Activity profiling works the same way. As you start to look at the profiles of customer orders, purchase orders, item activity, inventory levels, and so on, the creative juices begin to flow for everyone on the project team. Everyone on the project team starts making good decisions and generating new ideas.

A Picture is Worth 1,000 Words

When you see a picture of a mother coddling her newborn baby, you experience a thousand simultaneous thoughts. We are aiming for the same effect in warehouse activity profiling as we paint a picture of what is going on inside the warehouse. In profiling, we are trying to capture the activity of the warehouse in pictorial form so we can present the information to management and so we can make quick consensus decisions as a team.

You Can Drown in Your Own Profiles

One warning before we begin to profile the warehouse (as an engineer and logistics nerd, I fall into this trap a lot)—you can drown in your own profiles. Some people call this paralysis of analysis. If you are not careful, you can get so caught up in profiling that you forget to solve the problem. You have to be careful to draw the line and say, *that is enough.*

A full, yet minimum set of profiles required to plan and design warehouse operations follows. This profile set is a synthesis of profiles built in a wide variety of warehouse project settings. They are presented to you as an example of the set of profiles you should have to effectively plan and manage your warehouse operations. The profile set stems directly from the seven key planning and design issues in warehousing (see Table 2-1).

TABLE 2-1   Warehouse Design Issues and Related Profiles

Planning and Design Issue	Key Questions	Required Profile	Profile Components
1. Order picking and shipping process design	• Order batch size • Pick wave planning • Picking tour construction • Shipping mode disposition	Customer order profile	• Order mix distributions • Lines per order distribution • Lines and cube per order distribution
2. Receiving and putaway process design	• Receiving mode disposition • Putaway batch sizing • Putaway tour construction	Purchase order profile	• Order mix distributions • Lines per receipt distribution • Lines and cube per receipt distribution
3. Slotting	• Zone definition • Storage mode selection and sizing • Pick face sizing • Item location assignment	Item activity profile	• Popularity profile • Cube-movement/volume profile • Popularity-volume profile • Order completion profile • Demand correlation profile • Demand variable profile

Planning and Design Issue	Key Questions	Required Profile	Profile Components
4. Material transport systems engineering	• Material handling systems selection and sizing	Calendar-clock profile	• Seasonality profile • Daily activity profile
5. Warehouse layout and material flow design	• Overall warehouse flow design:U, S, I, or L flow • Relative functional locations • Building configuration	Activity relationship profile	• Activity relationship distribution
6. Warehouse sizing	• Overall warehouse space requirements	Inventory profile	• Item family inventory distribution • Handling unit inventory distribution
7. Level of automation and staffing	• Staffing requirements • Capital-labor substitution • Level of mechanization	Automation profile	• Economic factors distribution

2.2   CUSTOMER ORDER PROFILING

In general, material and information should flow through a warehouse to facilitate excellent customer service. What do customers really want from the warehouse? They want their orders filled. Then, the first thing we must understand to plan and design warehouse operations is the profile of customer orders.

A Warehouse in a Warehouse

Some customers place such high demands on a warehouse, represent such a large portion of the activity in the warehouse, and have such high customer service requirements that it may make sense to establish a separate area within the warehouse for a particular customer or business unit—a warehouse within the warehouse. For example, a major apparel manufacturer does so much business with JC Penney that they have a JC Penney warehouse within their warehouse. A major distributor of packaging does so much business with May Company, that they have a May Company warehouse within their warehouse for May Company shopping bags. Third-party warehousing takes the warehouse within a warehouse notion to an extreme. In public warehouses, aisles within the warehouse are dedicated to specific customers. In contract warehouses, the entire warehouse is devoted to the needs of a single customer.

As another example, many warehouses serve multiple business units under the same roof. This oftentimes is a major point of contention—the efficiency of shared resources versus business unit *control*. (Via clever design and intelligent warehouse management systems, you can have both.) For example, a large telecommunications company struggled through this trade-off recently. It historically served four or five different business units from the same warehouse. Reserve inventory was commingled. Unique forward picking areas were established for each business unit. In this case, the argument for *business unit* control won out. The major reason was the lack of adequate warehouse management systems and organizational support to enable the managers of the warehouse to offer each business unit a tailored warehousing program. At the opposite end of the spectrum is another telecommunications company that has perfected tailored warehousing programs for diverse business units housed in the same distribution center. The company is so proficient at warehousing that they are considering entering the third-party warehousing business for their industry.

In another example (see Figure 2-2), in a large publisher's distribution center, a central pool of reserve stock is used to support three distinct busi-

FIGURE 2-2   **Example of a warehouse within a warehouse concept.**

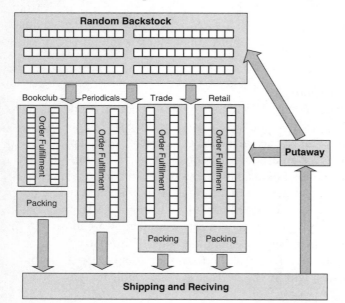

ness units—retail, trade, and periodicals. Each business unit has allocated/reserve inventory in the central warehouse and distinct forward picking zones to facilitate excellent customer service. The manager of each forward picking zone has a dotted line reporting relationship to the business unit to which his picking zone is reporting. The solid line reporting relationship is to the director of distribution. This is the best of both worlds— shared receiving resources, efficient handling of central inventory, dedicated forward picking lines, and shared shipping resources.

The warehouse within a warehouse design philosophy works because small warehouses, in general, have higher productivity and customer service performance than large warehouses (see Figure 3-3). The warehouse within a warehouse design philosophy enables us to divide and conquer the warehouse mission. Many of the customer order and item activity profiles are designed to identify opportunities to subdivide the entire warehouse operation into self-contained warehouse processing cells, virtual warehouses, or warehouses within the warehouse. This design approach is similar to that used in manufacturing, where manufacturing activity profiles are designed to specify flexible manufacturing cells inside a large factory.

Customer Order Profile

The customer order profile includes

- Order mix distributions
- Lines per order distribution
- Cube per order distribution
- Lines and cube per order distribution

The best way to explain each of these distributions and their interpretations is to review a series of examples.

Order Mix Distributions   There are a variety of order mix distributions that are helpful for plotting warehouse operating strategy. Three of the most helpful are the family mix distribution, the handling unit distribution, and the order increment distribution.

Family Mix Distribution   In many cases, the overall operating strategy of the warehouse is dictated by the *order mix,* the extent to which orders require items from multiple families of items. If the orders are pure, that is, tend to have just one of the families of items on them, then it is an early indicator that zoning the warehouse on that basis will create a virtual warehouse within the warehouse and will lead to good productivity and customer service.

FIGURE 2-3   Example of family mix distribution.

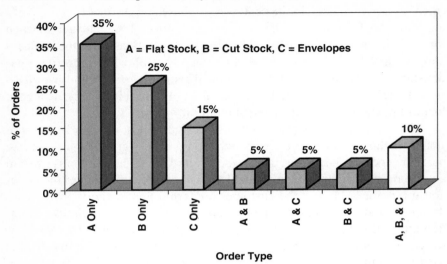

The family mix distribution in Figure 2-3 comes from a wholesale distributor of fine papers, copy/laser paper, and envelopes. Category A is a family of merchandise called flat stock. Printers make high-quality brochures from these flat stocks of fine papers. A carton of flat stock is about 30 inches long, 24 inches wide, and 9 inches deep. A carton weighs about 80 pounds. Category B is cut stock, basic 8 1/2 × 11-inch copier and laser printer paper. A carton of cut stock is about 24 inches long, 10 inches wide, and 10 inches deep. A carton weighs about 20 pounds. Category C is envelopes and labels —extremely small and lightweight merchandise.

In this example, we are trying to figure out if it makes sense to zone the warehouse by those three item families: flat stock, cut stock, and envelopes. If the orders are mixed, that is, flat stock, cut stock, and envelopes tend to appear together on customer orders, then in pallet building we would start with flat stock, put cut stock on top of that, and put envelopes on top of that. If that is the way we zone the warehouse, we may pay a big travel time penalty because we will have to travel across those zones or pass a pallet from one zone to the next.

If the orders are pure, that is, they tend to be completable out of just one item family, then zoning the warehouse along these lines will establish efficient warehouse processing cells, especially because products tend to be received into the warehouse as flat stock, cut stock, and envelope shipments.

In Figure 2-3, 35 percent of the orders can be completed out of flat stock alone, 25 percent of the orders can be completed out of cut stock alone, and 15 percent out of envelopes alone. The good news is that 75 percent (35 percent + 25 percent + 15 percent) of the orders can be completed out of a single item family suggesting that zoning the warehouse by item family will yield good productivity, customer service, and storage density performance.

Handling Unit Mix Distributions   The full/partial pallet mix distribution and the full/broken case mix distribution are two revealing handling unit mix distributions.

- **Full/Partial Pallet Mix Distribution**   With the full/partial pallet mix distribution, we try to determine if we need separate areas for pallet picking and case picking. In some warehouses, pallet and case picking are performed out of the same item location, aisle, and/or area of the warehouse. In general, it is a good idea to establish separate areas for pallet and case picking—replenishing a case picking line/area from a pallet reserve/picking area. This distribution simply helps reinforce the point and helps to identify warehouse within a warehouse opportunities.

  In Figure 2-4, 50 percent of the orders are completable out of partial pallet quantities, that is, just case picks; 30 percent of the orders are fillable from full pallet quantities, and the remaining 20 percent of the orders require both partial and full pallet quantities.

  Should we have a separate case picking and pallet picking area? If we did, would we pay a big penalty for mixed orders that require merging of the partial and full pallet portions of the order? No, we really won't. That only happens 20 percent of the time. For 80 percent of the orders, zoning based on pallet/case picking creates a warehouse within the warehouse. When the orders come into the warehouse management system, it should classify them immediately as a pallet pick order, a carton pick order, or a mixed order. For mixed orders, the warehouse management system should create a pallet portion, a case pick portion, and either pass the full pallet portion to the case pick area, or merge the case pick and pallet portions downstream from picking.

  You now begin to see how we can quickly address the major planning and design decisions by having the right information available to us in the right format.

- **Full/Broken Case Mix Distribution**   With this distribution (see Figure 2-5), we try to determine if we should create separate areas for

FIGURE 2-4   Example of full/partial pallet mix distribution.

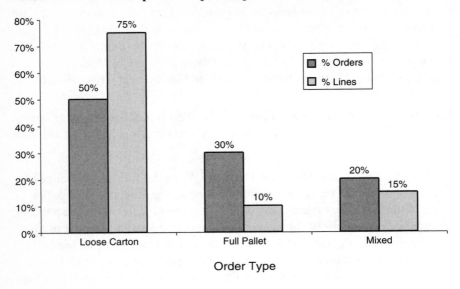

FIGURE 2-5   Example of full/broken case mix distribution.

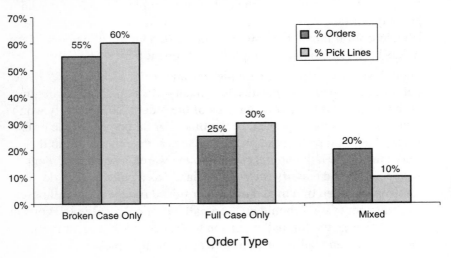

full and broken case picking. In some warehouses, full and broken case picking are performed out of the same item location, aisle, and/or area of the warehouse. In general, it is a good idea to establish separate areas for full and broken case picking—replenishing a broken case picking line/area from a case reserve/picking area. This distribution simply helps reinforce the point and helps to identify warehouse within a warehouse opportunities. As was the case with the pallet/case mix distribution in Figure 2-4, the distribution in Figure 2-5 indicates that only a small portion of the orders require both a full and broken case quantity. Hence, to create separate areas for full and broken case picking will yield two order completion zones with very little mixing between them.

Order Increment Distributions   With the order increment distribution (see Figure 2-6), we determine the portion of a unit load (in this case, a pallet) requested on a customer order. For example, suppose there are 100 cartons on a pallet and a customer orders 50 cartons. In that case, they ordered 50 percent of the pallet. If there are 80 cartons on a pallet and a customer orders 20, they ordered 25 percent of the pallet.

What do you notice that is unusual about this distribution? (In almost all of these distributions, the key insights are in the peaks and valleys.) Where are the peaks? The peaks are around 25 percent and 50 percent of a pallet.

Suppose there are 100 cartons on a pallet and a customer places an order for 100 cartons. Would you rather pick a full pallet or 100 individual

FIGURE 2-6   **Example of pallet order increment distribution.**

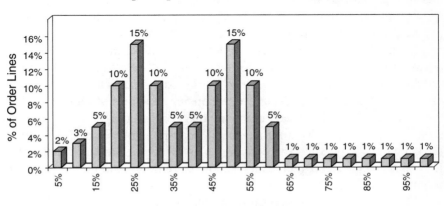

cartons? You didn't have to buy this book to figure out that you would prefer to pick a whole pallet at a time. That is not only good practice for you, but it is good practice for your customer as well. The customer would rather receive a full pallet quantity that they can handle in one unit load as opposed to having to handle 100 loose cartons.

Now, what operating decision should we make to take advantage of the distribution in Figure 2-6? Right, we should build some quarter- and half-pallet unit loads. Then, when a customer places an order for a quarter pallet, we have that unit load preconfigured. If a customer places an order for a half pallet, we have that unit load preconfigured.

How can we build half- and quarter-pallet unit loads? In this particular case, the manufacturing facility is attached to the warehouse. There is a palletizer that sits on the border, and all we have to do is set the palletizer to put a pallet in place about four times as often to build quarter pallets and twice as often to build half pallets. If the warehouse is not attached to manufacturing, the next best scenario is to have the supplier build the quarter- and half-pallet loads. If not the supplier, then we can preconfigure the unit loads at receiving.

Can we encourage people to order in half-, quarter-, and/or layer-quantity increments? Absolutely. In many cases, by simply making the pallet/layer quantities accurate and visible to the customer and the order entry personnel via the logistics information system, we can encourage the practice of ordering in preconfigured unit loads. We can further encourage the practice by offering price discounts designed around efficient handling increments. In this case, there was a representative from the sales organization on the cross-functional team who literally reset the price breaks on the quarter- and half-pallet quantities the next day.

The two potential downsides of preconfiguring subpallet unit loads are (1) the complexities of mixing the practice with FIFO rotation requirements and (2) the loss of storage density. For FIFO rotation, the warehouse management system should be able to track date and lot rotation within FIFO windows. I believe in many industries, FIFO requirements are named falsely as an impediment to world-class warehousing practices. As an example, I recently worked with a candy company that continued to hold out FIFO as a barrier to productivity improvements. I can remember a design meeting on Valentines Day when the company was receiving product for the Halloween season. Indeed, there can be some large time windows within FIFO requirements.

There will be some loss in storage density because a pallet worth of cartons may now have two or four pallets supporting it for some unit loads. For half-pallet quantities, we should be able to stack two halves in a full opening. For quarter pallets, we may need a row of openings that are 15 percent taller than the opening for singles. As a result, the loss in storage density should be less than 5 percent for the entire warehouse. The profile should also tell us the potential productivity yield associated with the new practice. If the yield is such that the loss in storage density is offset, the practice should be implemented. If not, the practice should not be implemented. The ability to make that decision objectively is the reason to have the profile.

With the case order increment distribution (see Figure 2-7), we determine the portion of a full carton that is requested on customer orders. For example, if there are 100 pieces in a carton and a customer orders 50, the customer ordered half the carton. What do you notice that is unusual about this distribution? In this case (see Figure 2-7), customers tend to order around half a carton and a quantity close to a full carton. As a result, we would like to set price breaks at a half carton (and create an inner pack for a half carton) and at a full carton to encourage customers who are almost ordering that quantity now to order in full carton increments.

The general principle is to prepackage in increments that people are likely to order in and to encourage customers to order in intelligent handling increments. A higher level principle is that the supplier should do as much as possible to help prepare products for picking and shipping. After we negotiate to have the supplier do as much for us as possible, then we should do as much as possible at the receiving dock to get product ready for shipping and packing, because it is at that moment that we have the largest time window available

FIGURE 2-7 **Example of case order increment distribution.**

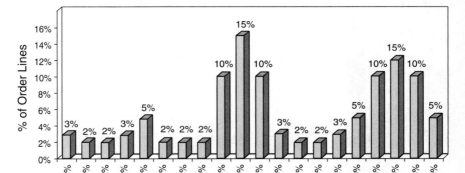

for picking/shipping preparation. As soon as an order drops for that product, the handling and preparation of the product should be at a minimum to meet the ever shrinking time window for product delivery.

Lines per Order Distribution   The lines per order distribution in Figure 2-8 indicates that 50 percent of the orders in the warehouse are for one line item, 15 percent for two, 15 percent for three to five, 10 percent for six to nine, and 10 percent for 10 or more. Where is the peak? It is around single line orders. This is not uncommon, especially in the mail order industry, in service parts logistics, or in cases where individual consumers or technicians are placing orders on the warehouse. We now need to consider the operating strategies that take advantage of this order profile.

First, *singles* may be backorders. Backorders are an excellent opportunity for cross-docking. Second, singles may be small, emergency orders. Those orders can be batched together for picking on single-line picking tours, and by printing single line orders in location sequence, we create very efficient picking tours. In addition, the order batches naturally zone the warehouse into zones defined by the length of the picking tour. Third, single line orders may also represent an opportunity to create a dynamic forward pick line. In this operating scenario, an automated look-ahead into the day's or shift's orders may yield a number of SKUs for which there is at least a full carton's worth of single line orders. Those SKUs can be batch picked and set up along fast pick-pack lines.

Another common lines per order distribution is the mirror image of Figure 2-8. The peak is around 10 plus lines per order. This is common in

FIGURE 2-8   Example of lines per order distribution.

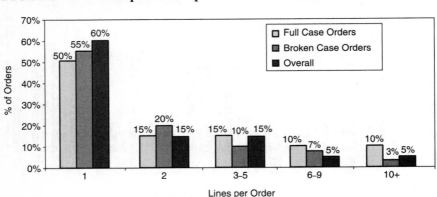

retail/grocery/dealer distribution where the customer is a retail store/grocery store/dealership. In that case, there is typically enough work to do within an order so that the order itself represents an efficient workset. Or, the order may be so large that it may be split across multiple order fillers for zone-wave picking.

Lines and Cube per Order Distribution   The lines and cube per order distribution (see Figure 2-9) brings together in one profile the critical information needed to define order picking strategy. It is a joint distribution that classifies all orders into *lines per* and *cube per* families. It illustrates the typical daily picking activity. In this example (see Figure 2-9), there are 176 orders with one line item and occupy less than a cubic foot of space. Those orders are probably candidates for a single operator to batch together for picking into compartmentalized picking carts, totes, or shipping containers. There is one order with more than 10 line items that occupies more than 20 cubic feet, about a third of a pallet. That order is a candidate for a single operator to pick to a pallet.

Purchase Order Profiling

The purchase order profile includes the same distributions (order mix distributions, lines per order distribution, and lines per order distribution) as the customer order profile. The only difference is that the activity is inbound instead of outbound. The purchase order profile is used to make the same

FIGURE 2-9   **Example of lines and cube per order distribution.**

Lines per Order	0-1	1-2	2-5	5-10	10-20	20+	Totals	% Orders	Total Lines	% Lines
			Cube per Order (Ft3)							
1	176	15	16	7	3	3	220	49%	220	17%
2-5	100	24	27	15	10	2	178	40%	623	47%
6-9	8	6	6	6	4	3	33	7%	248	19%
10+	2	1	1	6	4	1	15	3%	225	17%
Totals	286	46	50	34	21	9	446	100%	1,316	100%
% Orders	64%	10%	11%	8%	5%	2%	100%			
Total Cube	143	69	175	255	315	270	1,227			

batching and processing strategy decisions as was the customer order profile, except the batching and processing strategies are for receiving and putaway as opposed to order picking. Keep in mind that your purchase order is your supplier's customer order. The structure is the same, a list of line item numbers, descriptions, and quantities. The only difference is that the purchase order is inbound to your warehouse, and the customer order is outbound from your warehouse.

This chapter focuses on the customer order profile because a single receipt/putaway may represent many bin trips for order picking. All of the distributions that make up the purchase order profile will not be presented because the purchase order profile is the customer order profile in reverse. That is not to discourage you from creating it for your warehouse. In fact, it is a critical and revealing part of the warehouse activity profile.

2.3   ITEM ACTIVITY PROFILING

The item activity profile is used primarily to slot the warehouse, to decide for each item (1) what storage mode the item should be assigned to, (2) how much space the item should be allocated in the storage mode, and (3) where in the storage mode the item should be located. The item activity profile includes the following activity distributions:

- Popularity distribution
- Cube-movement/volume distribution
- Popularity-volume distribution
- Order completion distribution
- Demand correlation distribution
- Demand variability distribution

Again, the best way to describe each distribution and its interpretation is by example.

Item popularity distribution—close to the door, close to the floor.
Just like a minority of the people in the world have a majority of the wealth, a minority of the items in a warehouse generate a majority of the picking activity. The popularity distribution (sometimes called an ABC curve or a Pareto distribution) indicates the x percent of picks associated with y percent of the SKUs (ranked by descending popularity). Figure 2-10 is a classic popularity distribution indicating that the 10 percent of the most popular items represent 70 percent of the picking activity, the 50 percent of the most popular items represent 90 percent of the picking activity, and so on.

FIGURE 2-10 Example of item popularity distribution.

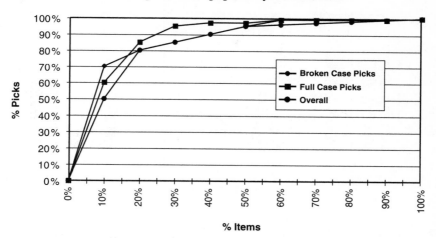

Dramatic breakpoints in the distribution may suggest item popularity families. For example, the top 5 percent of the items (Family A) may make up 50 percent of the picking activity, the next 15 percent of the items (Family B) may take us to 80 percent of the picking activity, and the remaining 80 percent of the items (Family C) cover the remaining picking activity. These families may in turn suggest three alternative storage modes: Family A in an automated, highly productive storage mode; Family B in a semi-automated, moderately productive picking mode, and Family C in a manual picking mode that offers high storage density. The family breakpoints may also suggest the location of the items within a storage mode—A items located in the *golden zone* (close to a travel aisle and/or at or near waist level), B items in the *silver zone*, and C items in the remaining spaces.

The overriding principle is to assign the most popular items to the most accessible warehouse locations. Unfortunately, many warehouse operators use the wrong measure of popularity. Some use dollar sales, some use usage, and some use the number of requests for the item. In the end, all of these are wrong. The number of requests for an item is the true measure of popularity; however, it is not enough information to assign items to storage modes or even to locate items within storage modes. The proper assignment of items to storage modes and allocation of space within the assigned storage mode is based on the popularity distribution and the cube-movement distribution. A cube-movement distribution example is presented in Figure 2-11. A joint popularity-cube-movement distribution follows in Figure 2-12. From

FIGURE 2-11   Example of cube-movement distribution.

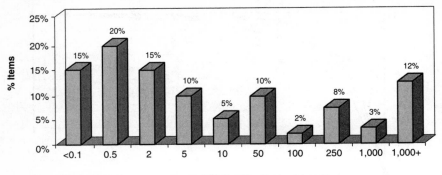

FIGURE 2-12   Example of popularity-cube-movement distribution for broken case picking.

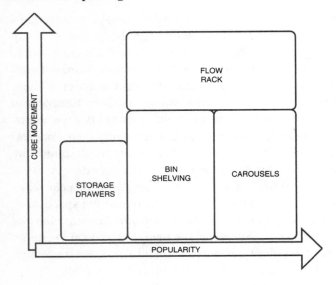

the joint popularity-cube-movement distribution, we can make appropriate slotting assignments.

Cube-Movement Distribution
The most revealing distribution for determining storage mode and space allocation decisions is the cube-movement (or volume) distribution. The cube-

movement distribution indicates the portion of items that fall into prespec-ified cube-movement ranges. If the prespecified ranges correspond to stor-age mode alternatives, then the cube-movement distribution will essentially solve the storage mode assignment problem. For example, in Figure 2-11, 15 percent of the items ship less than 0.1 cubic feet per month. Those items may be good candidates for storage drawers or bin shelving. At the other end of the distribution, we find 12 percent of the items that move more than 1,000 cubic feet (nearly 20 pallets) per month. Those items may be candi-dates for block stacking, double-deep rack, push-back rack, and/or pallet flow lanes. *The principle is to assign items to storage modes based on their cube-movement.*

Popularity-Cube-Movement Distribution

When done properly, slotting takes into account both the item popularity dis-tribution and the cube-movement distribution. These distributions can be combined into a joint distribution. An example popularity-cube-movement distribution for broken case picking is presented in Figure 2-12.

In the example, those items exceeding a certain cube-movement thresh-old are assigned to carton flow rack. Items with high cube-movement turnover need to be restocked frequently and need a larger storage location as compared to items with medium and low cube-movement. Hence, they need to be assigned to a storage mode that facilitates restocking and con-denses large storage locations along the pick line-carton flow rack. Items with low cube movement and high popularity are generating many picks per unit of space that they occupy and do not occupy much space along the pick line. They need to be in a highly productive picking mode. In this case, light directed carousels are recommended because the picking productivity is high and we can afford the carousels for items that do not need large storage hous-ings on the pick line and do not need to be restocked frequently. (Carousels do not lend themselves to restocking and are expensive per cubic foot of space.) Items with low popularity and low cube-movement cannot be justi-fiably housed in an expensive storage mode. Hence, they are candidates for bin shelving and modular storage drawers. Once the storage mode assign-ments have been made, the preference regions for each storage mode become their popularity-cube-movement distributions. Those items in the bottom right-hand portion of the distribution generate the most picking activ-ity per unit of space they occupy in the storage mode. Hence, they should be assigned to positions in the golden zone. Those items in the upper right-hand and lower left-hand generate a moderate number of picks per unit of space they occupy in the storage mode. Hence, they should be assigned to positions in the silver zone. Finally, those items in the upper left-hand quadrant of the distribution generate the fewest picks per unit of space they occupy, and they should be assigned positions in the bronze (least accessible) zone.

This example is not meant to make an end-all recommendation for slotting broken case picking systems. That depends on many other factors including the wage rate, the cost of space, the cost of capital, the planning horizon, and so on. Instead, this example is presented to illustrate how the popularity-cube-movement distribution is used in the slotting process. Once in place, the distribution provides most of the insights required for slotting the entire warehouse.

Item-Order Completion Distribution

The item-order completion distribution (see Figure 2-13) identifies small groups of items that can fill large groups of orders. Those small groups of items can often be assigned to small *order completion zones* in which the productivity, processing rate, and processing quality are two to five times better than that found in the general warehouse.

The item-order completion distribution is constructed by ranking the items from most to least popular. Beginning with the most popular item, then the two most popular items, then the three most popular items, and so on, the items are put against the order set to determine what portion of the orders a given subset of the items can complete. In this example, 10 percent of the

FIGURE 2-13   **Example item-order completion distribution.**

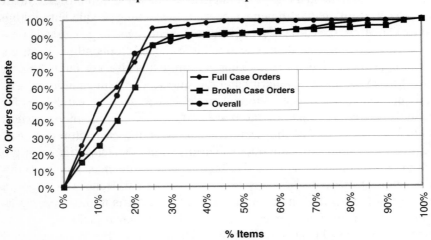

items can complete 50 percent of the orders. Suppose I walk into your warehouse and identify 10 percent of the items that can completely fill 50 percent of the orders. What would you do with those 10 percent? I hope you would create a warehouse within the warehouse or order completion zone for those 10 percent.

The design principle is similar to that used in agile manufacturing, where we look for small groups of parts that have similar machine routings. Those machines and those parts make up a small group technology cell wherein the manufacturing efficiency, quality, and cycle time are dramatically improved over those found in the factory as a whole.

I recently worked with a large media (compact discs, cassettes, videos, and so on) distributor and helped to identify 5 percent of its 4,000 SKUs that could complete 35 percent of the orders. We assigned those 5 percent to carton flow rack pods (three flow rack bays per pod, one operator per pod) at the front of the distribution center. Operators could pick-pack orders from the flow rack at nearly six times the overall rate of the distribution center. The distribution center has won its industry's productivity award for the last two years.

Demand Correlation Distribution

The demand correlation distribution (see Figure 2-14) indicates the affinity of demand between individual items and between families of items. Just like a minority of the items in a warehouse make up a majority of the picking activity, certain items in the warehouse tend to be requested together. In the example, pairs of items are ranked based on their frequency of appearing together on orders. We are looking for general patterns. In this case, we are examining data from a mail order apparel company. The first three digits represent the style of the item (that is, crew neck sweater, V-neck sweater, turtle neck shirt, pleated pants, and so on), the middle digit represents the size of the item (1=small, 2=medium, 3=large, 4=extra large), and the last digit represents the color (1=white, 2=black, 3=red, 4=blue, 5=green, and so on).

What do you think people tend to order together from this mail order apparel catalog operator? (I thought it would be shirts and pants that looked good together in the catalog.) What does the distribution in Figure 2-14 suggest? In this case, customers tend to order items of the same style and size together. The explanation is that customers tend to get comfortable with a certain style and tend to order in multiple colors to add variety to their wardrobe. Of course, they order the same size unless they will return one for fitting. This was a surprise to me. More importantly, it was a surprise to

FIGURE 2-14   Example of demand correlation distribution (style-size-color).

Item Number	Item Number	Pair Frequency
189-2-4	189-2-1	58
493-2-1	493-2-8	45
007-3-3	007-3-2	36
119-2-1	119-2-7	30
999-1-8	999-1-6	22
207-4-2	207-4-4	15
662-1-9	662-1-1	12
339-7-4	879-2-8	9
112-3-8	112-3-4	6

the marketing people. That is the most important reason to go through the profiling process—to surface the truth. (Unfortunately, our intuition about logistics issues is often off-base. The myriad of SKUs, order patterns, suppliers, and interdependent decisions make it difficult to form reliable intuition about logistics operations.)

How do we take advantage of this demand-correlation information in slotting the warehouse? We are looking for the lowest common denominator of correlation, the factor that will create the largest family of items. In this case, it is the size of the item. So, we zone the warehouse by item size first, creating a zone for the smalls, mediums, larges, and extra larges of all styles. Within each size area, we store items of the same style together, mixing colors within a style. This zoning strategy enables us to create picking tours based on size and style. As a result, order pickers can pick many items on short-distance picking tours. At the same time, we will manage congestion by spreading out the sizes. Golden zoning is used to store the most popular color for each style at or near waist level.

Demand Variability Distribution

The demand variability distribution (see Figure 2-15) indicates the standard deviation of daily demand for each item. Unfortunately, an item's daily demand is not predictable. During a recent project, we were trying to size the pick faces along a case picking line such that each pick face held a day's worth of stock. The motivator was to make sure that we did not need to restock a location during the day. The current design had the pick faces sized for an average day's demand, and the client could not figure out why they had to restock so many locations during the course of the day. I hope you see why. If the pick face is sized for the average day, unless the same quantity is picked every single day, there will be many days when the pick face is oversized and many days when the pick face is undersized, thus requiring a replenishment.

The real objective was to make sure that there was no need to restock during a picking shift (two pick shifts per day and one restocking shift per day). Hence, the pick face must be sized to accommodate the average day's demand plus enough to cover one standard deviation of demand for a 5 percent chance of restocking and two standard deviations of demand for a 1 percent chance of restocking. Once the pick faces were resized to accommodate this variability of demand, the restocking during the pick shift was virtually eliminated.

FIGURE 2-15   **Example of demand variability distribution.**

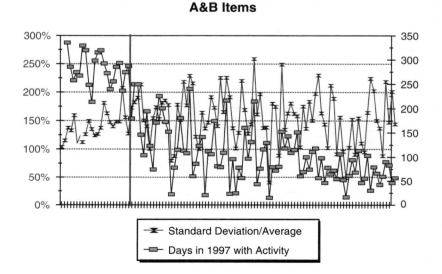

2.4   INVENTORY PROFILE

The inventory profile includes the item-family inventory distribution used to reveal opportunities for improved inventory management practices and the handling unit inventory profile used in storage systems planning.

Item-Family Inventory Distribution

The item-family inventory distribution indicates the amount of inventory on-hand by item popularity family. In this example from the textiles industry (see Figure 2-16), there are 40 million yards of product on-hand for A items (80 percent of sales and 5 percent of items), 20 million yards for B items (15 percent of sales and 15 percent of items), and 19 million yards for C items (5 percent of sales and 80 percent of items). A items turn 30 times per year, B items 10 times per year, and C items four times per year. What's wrong with this picture?

I receive a lot of phone calls that begin with a client complaining about the lack of space in his or her warehouse. *More often than not, the problem is not too little space, but too much inventory.* This profile helps us identify the source of the inventory problem. As is true in the example, most companies have too little A inventory (backorders and customers screaming for those products) and too much C inventory (obsolete stock that nobody wants and nobody has the courage to discard). By drawing the picture, we can at

FIGURE 2-16   **Example of item-family inventory distribution.**

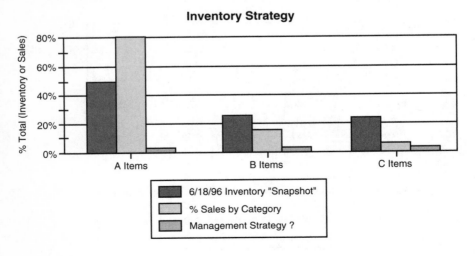

least illustrate the magnitude of the problem to management and present a list of "problem" items for their review.

In some cases, the C items should be removed from inventory. The problem may be the lack of a formal item inventory review program. In this case, the profile helps identify the candidates for removal.

In many cases, however, you are forced to house the C items. One example is in the service parts business, where you may be required to support a certain model number in the field for up to 5, 10, even 20 years. Another example is in retailing, when some key C items protect the sales of the A and B items. On a recent project in the grocery industry, the chairman of the company was presented with a recommendation to eliminate the C items from inventory. Let's pause and consider the consequences. How many items do you buy on your weekly trip to the grocery store to restock the kitchen cabinets? Say it's 50 items. In that case, there is at least a 70 percent chance that one of those 50 items is a C item. Why did you go to that grocery store? In the case of this grocery chain, it was probably because they stocked that C item. Otherwise, you could and would shop at a warehouse store.

Even though you may not be able to eliminate the C inventory in some cases, you can at least be efficient in the way you store and pick the items. To conserve space, you may want to store the C inventory in dense, high-rise racking or on the second or third level of a mezzanine. To get good productivity at the same time, you may want to batch pick the C-item pickline and locate the batch in a dedicated location along the forward pick line or introduce the batch into an automated sortation system.

Handling Unit Inventory Distribution

The item-family inventory distribution is not very useful for storage systems design because the information is not presented in material handling terms (that is, pallets, cases, eaches, and so on). This is a common problem with most corporate data used in planning warehouse operations—the data is expressed in terms of dollars, pounds, pieces, days of supply, turns, and so on. Though useful for business planning purposes, the data is not very helpful for planning and managing warehouse operations. That is another motivation for the profiling exercise—to give the managers and designers of the warehouse operations a presentation of the activity of the warehouse in their terminology.

In this example (see Figure 2-17), we convert the item-family inventory distribution into a distribution describing on-hand inventory in terms of pallets of merchandise on-hand. As a result, we can recommend the appropriate mix of pallet storage modes. For example, the 10,000 SKUs with less

FIGURE 2-17   Example of handling unit inventory distribution.

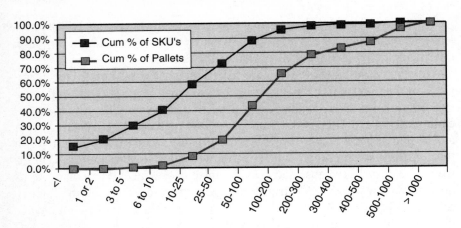

Number of Pallets on Hand

than a pallet of inventory on-hand should probably be stored in shelving or decked racking. The 1,200 SKUs that have one or two pallets on-hand should probably be stored in single-deep pallet rack. The 500 SKUs that have three to five pallets on-hand should probably be stored in double-deep and/or push-back rack. The remaining SKUs, those with more than 10 pallets on-hand, should probably be stored on the floor in deep-block stacking lanes, in drive in/thru rack, and/or in pallet flow lanes.

2.5   CALENDAR-CLOCK PROFILE
The calendar-clock profile includes a seasonality distribution and a daily activity distribution. The distributions are designed to reveal peaks and valleys in warehouse activity so that material handling systems can be properly sized and so that proper staff scheduling programs can be designed.

Seasonality Distribution
The seasonality distribution (see Figure 2-18) indicates the peaks and valleys in inventory levels as well as receiving, shipping, and returns activity. Because storage systems need to be sized to accommodate near-peak inventory levels, and material handling systems need to be sized to accommodate near-peak activity levels, it is critical to identify peak inventory and activ-

FIGURE 2-18   **Example of seasonality distribution.**

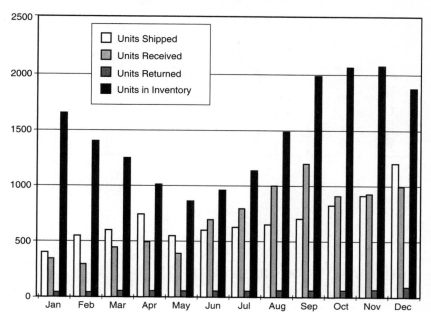

ity levels. The example is typical of retail distribution with receipts peaking in August/September, inventory peaking in September/October, shipping peaking in October/November, and returns peaking in January. A distribution like this also indicates an opportunity for workforce shifting by moving the extra staff required for receiving in August/September to shipping in October/November to returns handling in January. (In the extreme, an employee could receive an item, put it away for storage, pick it for shipping, and return it into the warehouse.) With the seasonality distribution in hand, a popular rule of thumb for planning purposes is to design material handling systems to accommodate the average day of the peak week.

Daily Activity Distribution

The daily activity distribution (see Figure 2-19) indicates hourly peaks and valleys in receiving, storage, picking, and shipping activity. Material handling systems should be designed for peak activity periods, and offsetting peaks represent opportunities for shift staggering and interdepartment workforce shifting.

FIGURE 2-19   Example of daily activity distribution.

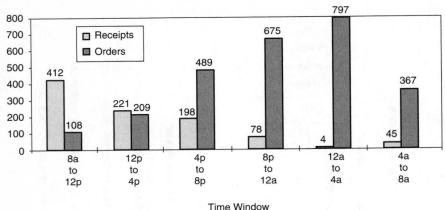

2.6   ACTIVITY RELATIONSHIP PROFILE

The activity relationship profile and distribution (see Figure 2-20) reveals the interfunctional and interprocess relationships in the warehouse. It is used to suggest the location of processes and functions relative to one another in a block layout. In the example, we simply record under each interprocess relationship the importance of locating the processes adjacent to one another. For example, it is critical that reserve storage be adjacent to receiving staging for efficient putaway (of course, receiving staging would be eliminated in a world-class warehouse).

2.7   INVESTMENT PROFILE

The investment profile indicates the cost and operating parameters necessary to make design and investment decisions. The profile includes the

- Wage rate (dollar per hour)
- Cost of space (dollar per square foot per year)
- Cost of capital (percent per year)
- Required ROI and/or payback period (percent or years)
- Working days per year (days per year)
- Planning horizon (years)

Design and investment decisions depend heavily on the investment profile. For example, in the auto industry, it is not uncommon for warehouse

FIGURE 2-20   **Example of activity relationship profile.**
Source: Naval Supply Systems Command

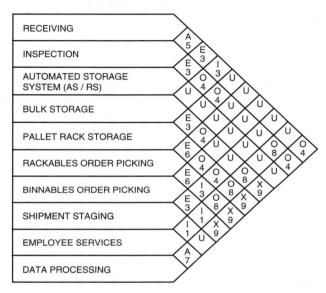

REASONS FOR IMPORTANCE

1. Supervision
2. Safety
3. Material flow
4. Work flow
5. Material control
6. Equipment proximity
7. Shared spaced
8. Employee Health and Safety
9. Security

PROXIMITY IMPORTANCE

A. Absolutely necessary
E. Especially important
I. Important
O. Ordinary closeness
U. Unimportant
X. Undesirable

operators to make $30 an hour. It is much easier to justify highly automated systems in that environment than in one where nonunion operators are making $7 to $12 per hour. It is much easier to justify high-density storage systems (such as, vertical carousels, mezzanines, storage drawers, and ASRS) when the cost of space is $20 to $50 per square foot per year than in the case of a recent project where a 15 year lease is signed for $2.25 per square foot per year. It is much easier to justify highly automated systems when the cost of capital is low (2 percent to 5 percent), when the required return-on-investment is low (7 percent to 12 percent), and when the required payback period is extended (three to five years). (We do not run into many of those situations in America. Those economic justification conditions are more common in Japan and parts of Europe. That is why the level of automation in warehousing and distribution in Japan and those parts of Europe is so much higher than that found in the United States.)

2.8 SUMMARY

By now, I hope you have experienced the power of profiling. If the warehouse activity profile is constructed and presented properly, the design and plan for the warehouse should literally jump off the pages of the profile. In the hands of experienced experts, a thorough profile should and can yield an accurate warehouse concept design in as little as half a day.

It may appear that profiling is a lot of work. It is. However, it is the work necessary to insure an accurate plan and design for the warehouse. Our clients are often impatient in the profiling phase of a project, anxiously wanting to get to the creative and design phases of the project. Then, once the profile is in place, they often are left with an anticlimactic feeling because the design follows so quickly from the profile.

Remember, there is no other time during the project life cycle—profile, conceptualize, design, implement, and maintain—that design changes are less expensive and the opportunity for improvement greater than during the profiling and conceptualizing phases of a project. Once you leave those phases, you need to be completely confident that you have made the right planning and design decisions based on thorough and objective considerations of the alternatives. Turning back or second guessing at that point is a high penalty to pay for impatience with the profiling process.

Finally, some bad news. As soon as the warehouse activity profile has been created, it changes. Hence, once initiated, the profiling process should never end. In fact, once initiated, warehouse activity profiling should never end. World-class warehouse management systems support continuous warehouse activity profiling, which in turn support continuous warehouse problem solving.

3

MEASURING AND BENCHMARKING WAREHOUSE PERFORMANCE

IN WAREHOUSE ACTIVITY PROFILING, we diagnosed the problems in the current operations and revealed a variety of opportunities for process improvement. In benchmarking against world-class standards, we set world-class performance, practice, and infrastructure goals for the warehouse operations. The goals have to be set at or above world-class standards because the definition of world-class improves continuously. To set goals below world-class insures that when we get to the goals we set, we will be at least as far behind as we currently are.

The benchmarking and goal setting process described here also permits the quantitative assessment of the opportunity for improvement in productivity, shipping accuracy, inventory accuracy, dock-to-stock time, warehouse order cycle time, and storage density. The benchmarking and goal setting process yields an estimate of an annual benefit related to the quantified opportunity for improvement. With that annual benefit (dollars per year) in hand, and in relation to the corporate required payback period, an estimate of the affordable investment available for process improvements is easily computed. This estimate further defines the possible alternatives and resources available for process improvements.

Section 1 is an introduction to benchmarking and how it is applied to warehousing and distribution operations. Section 2 outlines recommended warehouse performance metrics. Section 3 describes *Warehouse Performance Gap Analysis* (WPGA), a formal methodology for assessing the performance of warehouse operations in productivity, accuracy, response time, storage density, and level of mechanization. WPGA can and should be used for setting project goals, justifying project expenditures, and choosing benchmarking partners. Section 4 presents the *warehouse performance index* (WPI), a single-score indicator of total warehouse performance. The WPI is related to three key warehouse design factors—workforce demographics, warehouse size, and the level of mechanization. Section 5 shares do's and don'ts for warehouse automation projects. Section 6 summarizes the chapter.

3.1 BENCHMARKING WAREHOUSE OPERATIONS

A benchmark is typically a quantitative assessment of some aspect of performance of an enterprise. Benchmarking is the process of gathering and sharing those assessments and developing an improvement plan of action based on the assessment. The process of benchmarking was popularized by the Xerox Corporation in the late 1980s and has been successfully applied to a variety of business functions and industries. The process is a key component of total quality management and there now exists an International Benchmarking Clearinghouse supported by over 100 major corporations.

The three perspectives of benchmarking are internal, external, and competitive. Internal benchmarking is focused on the operations of a single company. External benchmarking looks outside the firm's industry. Competitive benchmarking looks at firms conducting business in the same industry. Examples of internal benchmarking, external benchmarking, and competitive benchmarking follow.

Internal Benchmarking

I have learned the hard way that the best way to explain benchmarking is through examples. This example of internal logistics benchmarking is from Gillette.

Gillette   Gillette's Latin American operations include manufacturing and distribution facilities in Mexico, Chile, Brazil, Colombia, Argentina, Venezuela, Ecuador, and Peru. Each year, the logistics managers at each operation are measured against 12 key logistics performance indicators, including shipping accuracy, inventory accuracy, inventory turns, fill rate, DC productivity, DC storage density, order cycle time, and perfect order percentage. There is a friendly competition among the group for the annual prize in each category and for the overall logistics performance award. Most importantly, the winner in each category is required to teach the group how he or she achieved that success in the previous year. In the course of this process, each operation is improved in every area.

External Benchmarking

Excellent examples of external benchmarking from Xerox and SBC follow.

Xerox Service Parts   Xerox Corporation recently embarked on a major distribution network reconfiguration. The reconfiguration included a review of the number, location, and design of all finished goods and service parts distribution facilities. In order to develop highly productive conceptual designs for their distribution centers, Xerox arranged tours of a variety of distribution facilities operating in other industries. During each site visit, Xerox and the host company exchanged information concerning the performance and practices of their distribution facilities and discussed the lessons learned by the host company in the design and operation of their facilities. Xerox agreed to host representatives from their benchmarking partners at their new operations once they were complete.

In order to quickly assess the overall performance of each facility on their tour, the logistics engineers from Xerox derived a simple measure of the performance of each distribution facility—the ratio of the annual of lines shipped from the facility to the annual labor hours expended in the facility. Simply, the lines shipped per person-hour. Those facilities with high scores were scrutinized and revisited to insure that the practices in place at those facilities were incorporated in the design of Xerox's new distribution facility.

Because of its excellent customer service and DC operations performance, the focal point for Xerox during the benchmarking exercise became L.L. Bean. Many of the processes in place at L.L. Bean's distribution center were incorporated into the Xerox design. The process worked because today Xerox enjoys a world-class rating in DC operations for service parts, and its Chicago service parts DC was recently recognized with *Modern Materials Handling's* annual productivity achievement award.

The Xerox case study is a classic example of external benchmarking because Xerox looked outside its own industry for benchmarking partners. That external perspective is critical to the success of the benchmarking exercise. First, most of the breakthroughs in logistics performance and practice have occurred across industry lines. For example, *efficient consumer response* (ECR) in the grocery industry is a take-off on *continuous flow replenishment* (CFR) from the electronics industry. CFR is a take-off on *quick-response* (QR) championed by Milliken in the textiles industry. QR is a take-off on *just-in-time* (JIT) from the Japanese automotive industry. Another example is the use of carousels in DC operations. Carousels were popularized in dry cleaning and office operations long before they made their way into warehousing. Second, it is typically quite difficult to gain the cooperation necessary to do the benchmarking process justice when the partners are within the same industry. Third, by benchmarking just within your own industry, you may establish yourself as the leader in your industry. However, if your industry is not proficient at logistics, you will be the best of a mediocre lot, or as one of my colleagues calls it, the queen of the hogs.

Just as important as the need to benchmark externally is the need to benchmark with *logistically similar* partners. In internal and competitive benchmarking, the similarities are obvious. However, in external benchmarking, it is more difficult to identify logistically similar operations. In the case of Xerox and L.L. Bean, they are logistically similar because their average order value is about the same, their average order cube is about the same, the average number of items on an order is about the same, they handle roughly the same transaction volume, and they carry roughly the same number of SKUs, and so on. To the extent your external benchmarking partner is logistically similar to you, your benchmarking partnership will be successful.

SBC SBC (formerly Ameritech and Southwestern Bell) is one of the nation's largest telecommunications providers. SBC's director of materials management was recently challenged by the CEO to reduce the cost of logistics in the company by 20 percent while maintaining and/or improving customer service levels. No additional moneys or resources for additional staff, systems, and/or consultants accompanied the challenge. The director in this case is a very clever gentleman. He conjectured that many of his colleagues in industry had been given similar charges by their management. He was right.

SBC, John Deere, United Stationers, and Exel Logistics recently completed one of the nation's most successful logistics benchmarking partnerships. The partnership was established from the response to invitations sent to companies with reputations for superior warehousing and distribution performance. Companies responding positively to the invitation were reviewed for competitive status, openness to sharing information, logistics similarity, and sensitivity to confidential information. After this filtering step, these four

progressive companies were left to the business of distribution performance enhancement.

This process of selecting benchmarking partners was critical to the success of this and to any benchmarking partnership. As SBC learned, an excellent benchmarking partner is

- Strong in the areas where you are weak and vice-versa
- Sensitive to confidentiality requirements
- Willing to admit weakness and share lessons learned
- Willing to admit strengths and share successes
- Open-minded
- Logistically similar
- Operating in a different industry and perhaps a different country

The formal benchmarking program began with an initiation meeting at SBC's South Bend, Indiana distribution center. During that first meeting, the group shared expectations and concerns, toured the DC operations, and developed a questionnaire to facilitate the comparison of the four diverse distribution operations. Each company was enabled to submit 12 questions for the questionnaire. As a result, the questionnaire included 48 questions concerning logistics performance and practices. The next step was the collection and analysis of the questionnaire responses. Because SBC called the partnership together, it served as the champion for scheduling meetings and compiling and reporting data.

The team convened three months later at John Deere's top performing distribution operation to review the operations there and to discuss the results of the survey. Next, based on the survey results and a vote of the participating companies, each company was assigned a topic to educate the members on. For example, John Deere's work measurement and safety program is world-renowned. As a result, John Deere was asked to teach the group its capabilities in work measurement and safety. SBC's excellence in customer service was readily evident from the survey. It was charged with teaching the group its customer service secrets. United Stationer's productivity was dominant. It was asked to share its productivity secrets. Exel's quality performance stood out and that became the focus of its presentations to the group. Three months later, the group convened again at United Stationer's top performing facility to review the operations there and to teach each other their secrets of success and lessons learned. The year-long process brought improved performance for each company as well as life long contacts for each participant in the team.

Competitive Benchmarking

Not long after the merger of two of the nation's largest wholesale distributors of healthcare supplies, a new vice president of distribution was brought in to oversee the newly merged distribution network. The network included over 30 distribution centers ranging in size from 50,000 to 500,000 square feet. Because the new vice president was not familiar with the industry's distribution performance, his first management initiative was to commission an assessment of the company's distribution performance as it compared to major competitors. The survey was facilitated by a large consulting organization and included data related to labor productivity measured in units shipped per man-hour, distribution cost as a percentage of sales, inventory turns, accuracy, and so on. The results of the survey quickly illustrated the strengths and weaknesses of the company's distribution performance and immediately identified a series of improvement projects.

Traditional Benchmarking Performance Metrics

Each of these case studies is an example of how the now common management process called benchmarking is applied in warehousing and distribution. As illustrated in these case studies, the focal and starting point for the benchmarking process has traditionally been the comparison of quantitative performance measures. For warehousing and distribution functions, the high-profile performance dimensions are operating cost, typically measured as warehousing and/or distribution cost as percent of sales, and operating productivity, typically measured in units (lines, orders, cases, pieces, pallets, pounds, and so on) handled per person-hour. (Renewed emphasis on customer service and quality have raised response time and shipping accuracy as critical measures.)

Though these measures act as good discussion starters, extreme caution should be used in the interpretation of performance based solely on them. For example, warehousing and distribution cost as a percentage of sales varies directly and widely with product pricing and sales volume—aspects of the operation that are usually outside the control of warehouse and distribution management. Cost as a percentage of sales figures also vary widely across industries. Example industry averages for logistics cost as a percentage of sales are presented in Tables 3-1 and 3-2. Warehousing costs can range from 10 percent to 50 percent of total logistics cost.

Warehousing unit costs can also be misleading as a performance benchmark. Annual warehousing cost (see Table 3-3) can be easily computed as the sum of the cost of the three major warehouse resources: labor, space, and systems (material handling, storage, and information handling).

TABLE 3-1   Definition and Composition of Logistics Costs

Cost Category	Cost as a % of Sales	Cost Per Hundred Weight
Transportation	3.31%	$11.93
Warehousing	2.03%	$10.96
Inventory carrying	1.82%	$ 9.86
Customer service and order processing	0.56%	$ 4.04
Administration	0.39%	$ 2.13
Other	0.19%	$ .66
TOTAL	7.93%	$37.64

Source: Herb Davis Associates

TABLE 3-2   Logistics Costs as a Percentage of Sales for Various Industries

Industry Segment	Logistics Costs as a % of Sales	Logistics Costs per Hundred Weight Shipped
Manufacturing	7.77%	$33.36
Industrial products	7.60%	$39.39
Consumer goods	7.82%	$31.38
Grocery	7.99%	$15.19
Food and beverage	8.49%	$ 8.22
General merchandise	7.44%	$38.22
Pharmaceuticals	4.31%	$86.00
Wholesalers	11.68%	$44.11
Retailers	5.34%	$86.15

Source: Herb Davis Associates

Annual labor cost is simply the annual hours worked per year multiplied by the wage rate. Annual space cost is the square footage occupied multiplied by the annual cost of space. Annual systems cost is the systems investment cost multiplied by the annual amortization/depreciation rate.

Again, remember that we are building a report card to assess the management and design of the warehouse. What influence do the managers and designers have on the wage rate? Little or none; the wage rate is a function

TABLE 3-3   Annual Warehousing Cost Computations

Resource	Consumption Measure	Consumption Cost
Labor	Person-hours per year	Wage rate (dollars per person-hour)
Space	Square feet occupied	Cost of space (dollars per square foot per year)
Material and information handling systems	Investment (dollars)	Amortization rate (percent per year)

of the availability of labor in the area and whether the operation is unionized or not. What influence do the managers and designers have on the cost of space? Little or none; the cost of space is a function of the availability of space and the prevailing cost of utilities and insurance. What influence do the managers and designers have on the annual amortization/depreciation rate? Again, little or none; it is determined by the accountants and financial analysts based on prevailing interest rates and the cost of capital. How well does the annual warehouse operating cost assess the designers and managers of the building as compared with the designers and managers of other operations? Potentially, not very well.

Now, consider the resources consumed. How much influence do the designers and managers have over the amount of labor consumed, the amount of space occupied, and the systems investment? Everything. In fact, the design and integration of those resources ultimately determine the performance of the warehouse. The performance in turn determines the cost of the operation. As a result, our benchmarking and goal setting methodology is focused on the consumption of warehouse resources—people, space, and systems—to meet the mission of the warehouse: shipping perfect (right products(s), right quality, on time, damage-free, right paperwork) orders and storing product efficiently.

3.2   WAREHOUSE PERFORMANCE MEASURES

In our methodology, the warehouse is accountable to the same competitive indicators the business is held to. Businesses compete on the basis of financial, productivity, quality, and cycle time performance. It is critical to hold the warehouse accountable to these business measures, because even private warehouses are, in effect, in business competition with third-party warehousers who are in the business of warehousing. If the private warehousing enterprise is not competitive with potential third-party providers, then the private operator should reconsider its justification for being in the warehousing business. The flip side is that if the private operator is a world-class warehouse operator, then the opportunity is available to turn the warehousing operations into profit-generating, third-party operations for the industry and/or other industries. One telecommunications provider has become so dominant in their logistics practices, that it is creating a third-party subsidiary to serve the industry.

Warehouse Financial Performance
In financial performance, we recommend that each warehouse establish a warehouse activity-based costing program. An example appears in Figure 3-1. In the example, a cost for each warehousing activity (receipt, putaway, store, pick, ship, and load) is established. The activity costs become the basis for comparing third-party warehousing proposals, budgeting, measuring improvement, and menu-based pricing for warehousing services.

FIGURE 3-1   Warehouse activity based costing example.
Source: LRI's Warehouse Scoreboard

	Labor Cost	Space Cost	MHS Cost	WMS Cost	Total Cost	Cost per Transaction	
Receiving	$ 1,963,055	$ 238,125	$ 569,820	$ 218,333	$ 2,989,333	$ 1.38	$ per receipt
Putaway	$ 1,090,534	$ -	$ 416,000	$ 240,333	$ 1,746,867	$ 3.56	$ per line
Storage	$ 999,640	$ 1,933,250	$ 1,650,710	$ 123,833	$ 4,707,433	$ 86.93	$ per SKU
Picking	$ 1,946,966	$ -	$ 1,830,782	$ 161,833	$ 3,939,581	$ 1.10	$ per line
Consolidation	$ 287,188	$ 100,500	$ 135,000	$ 38,333	$ 561,021	$ 61.45	$ per load
Delivery	$ 68,225	$ 50,000	$ 69,000	$ 38,333	$ 225,558	$ 24.71	$ per load
Marketing	$ 3,534,218	$ 105,000	$ 222,200	$ 113,833	$ 3,975,251	$ 0.22	$ per piece
Returns	$ 68,225	$ 99,250	$ 6,000	$ 113,000	$ 286,475		
Total	**$ 9,958,052**	**$ 2,526,125**	**$ 4,899,512**	**$ 1,047,831**	**$18,431,520**	**$ 368.63**	**$ per line**
% of Total	54.03%	13.71%	26.58%	5.68%	100.00%		
Cost/Sales	4.05%	1.03%	1.99%	0.43%	7.49%		
Cost/Order	$ 199.16	$ 50.52	$ 97.99	$ 20.96	$ 368.63		
Cost/Case	$ 4.58	$ 1.16	$ 2.25	$ 0.48	$ 8.47		
Cost/Line	$ 2.79	$ 0.71	$ 1.37	$ 0.29	$ 5.16		
Cost/Piece	$ 0.11	$ 0.03	$ 0.06	$ 0.01	$ 0.21		
Cost/CF	$ 2.77	$ 0.70	$ 1.36	$ 0.29	$ 5.12		
Cost/Pound	$ 0.35	$ 0.09	$ 0.17	$ 0.04	$ 0.64		
Cost/SKU	$ 183.89	$ 46.65	$ 90.48	$ 19.35	$ 340.37		

LOGISTICS RESOURCES INTERNATIONAL, INC.

In this particular analysis, the cost of storing and handling an item in the warehouse for a year was estimated to be $340.37. This warehouse managed over 70,000 items, 40,000 of which did not yield $340.37 in sales per year, not even enough to cover their storage and handling costs. Needless to say, the finding was taken up with the marketing area and a SKU reduction ensued.

Warehouse Productivity Performance

The most popular and traditional warehouse performance measure is productivity. The formal definition of productivity is the ratio of the output of a resource to the inputs required to achieve that output. We recommend that our clients monitor the productivity and utilization of the key assets in the warehouse—labor, space, material handling systems, and warehouse management systems. We typically measure overall labor productivity as the ratio of units, orders, lines, or weight shipped out of the warehouse to the number of hours spent in operating, supervising, and managing the warehouse. Used in isolation, labor productivity can be a very misleading indicator. For example, an operation may have a very high labor productivity achieved via inappropriately high investments in material and information handling systems.

Storage density, the ratio of the amount of inventory storage capacity to the square footage in the warehouse, is our recommended productivity indicator for floorspace. It is normally expressed as the value, cube, pieces, or positions of inventory that can be accommodated per square foot. In addition, we suggest that each warehouse continuously monitor the percent of available storage locations that are occupied (location utilization) and the percent of available storage cube that is occupied (cube utilization). Unlike productivity and accuracy, where the objective is clearly to maximize the indicator, the storage density should be within a world-class range. Storage density that is too high may indicate overcrowded conditions and storage density that is too low may indicate underutilized facilities.

Warehouse Quality Performance

There are four key quality indicators for warehouse performance—two for inbound handling and two for outbound handling:

- **Putaway accuracy** The percent of items putaway correctly
- **Inventory accuracy** The percent of warehouse locations without inventory discrepancies
- **Picking accuracy** The percent of order lines picked without errors

- **Shipping accuracy**   The percent of order lines shipped without errors

The best warehouse operators in the United States have shipping accuracy at or near 99.97 percent. The best warehouse operators in Japan have shipping accuracy at or near 99.997 percent, an order of magnitude improvement. Learning these gaps and experiencing the sense of urgency to close the gap are two of the most valuable results of an external benchmarking process.

Warehouse Cycle Time Performance
For cycle time, we recommend the warehouse track performance in two key areas:

- **Dock-to-Stock Time (DTS)**   The elapsed time from when a receipt arrives on the warehouse premises until it is ready for picking or shipping
- **Warehouse Order Cycle Time (WOCT)**   The elapsed time from when an order is released to the warehouse floor until it is picked, packed, and ready for shipping

Table 3-4 is a summary of the recommended indicators.

3.3   WAREHOUSE PERFORMANCE GAP ANALYSIS

Warehouse performance gap analysis (WPGA) is our benchmarking methodology for assessing the utilization of warehouse infrastructure (people, space, and systems) in meeting the mission of the warehouse (shipping perfect orders and consolidating inventory). We often assess our client's performance in the form of a warehouse performance gap analysis (see Figure 3-2) indicating to the client their standing versus world-class norms in the key performance indicators and the cost savings that are available if the gaps can be closed (see Figure 3-3). The radials (or spokes) represent the key performance indicators for the operations. The outer ring defines world-class performance.

In the example in Figure 3-2, the warehouse performance indicators are productivity (lines per hour), storage density (case storage capacity per square foot), shipping accuracy (percent lines shipped in error), inventory accuracy, dock-to-stock time, and order preparation time. In the example in Figure 3-3, the annual savings opportunity for attaining world-class warehousing is $1.8 million per year, leading to a justifiable investment in a world-class warehousing initiative of $2.7 million.

TABLE 3-4 Warehouse Key Performance Indicators (WKPIs)

	Financial	Productivity	Utilization	Quality	Cycle Time
Receiving	Receiving cost per receiving line	Receipts per man-hour	% Dock door utilization	% Receipts processed accurately	Receipt processing time per receipt
Putaway	Putaway cost per putaway line	Putaways per man-hour	% Utilization of putaway labor and equipment	% Perfect putaways	Putaway cycle time (per putaway)
Storage	Storage space cost per item	Inventory per square foot	% Locations and cube occupied	% Locations without inventory discrepancies	Inventory days on hand
Order picking	Picking cost per order line	Order lines picked per man-hour	% Utilization of picking labor and equipment	% Perfect picking lines	Order picking cycle time (per order)
Shipping	Shipping cost per customer order	Orders prepared for shipment per man-hour	% Utilization of shipping docks	% Perfect shipments	Warehouse order cycle time
TOTAL	Total cost per order, line, and item	Total lines shipped per total man-hour	% Utilization of total throughput and storage capacity	% Perfect warehouse orders	Total warehouse cycle time = Dock-to-stock time + Warehouse order cycle time

FIGURE 3-2   Example of warehouse performance gap analysis.

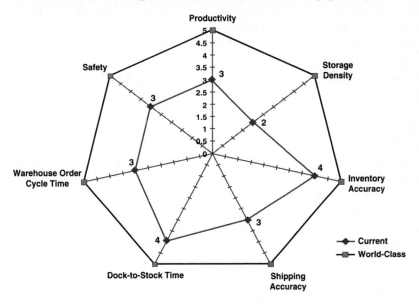

FIGURE 3-3   Warehouse Financial Opportunities Assessment

	Productivity	Storage Density	Inventory Accuracy	Shipping Accuracy	Dock-to-Stock Time	Warehouse Order Cycle Time	Safety
Annual Volume	360,000 lines/PH	29,000 SKUs	26,000 locations	360,000 lines/year	$120,000,000 on-hand inventory	$120,000,001 on-hand inventory	
Current Performance	4 lines/PH	1.89 SF/SKU	85% % locations	99.7% % lines	48 hours	24 hours	5 accidents/year
Current Resource Requirement	90,000 person-hours	54,810 SF	3,900 locations	1,080 locations			
World-Class Performance	6 lines/PH	1 SF/SKU	95% % locations	99.97% % lines	24 hours	12 hours	1 accidents/year
World-Class Resource Requirement	60,000 person-hours	29,000 SF	1,300 locations	108 lines/year			
Resource Savings	30,000 person-hours	25,810 SF	2,600 locations	972 lines/year	24 hours	12 hours	4
Rate	$25 $/PH	$11 $/SF *Yr.	$100 $/location	$300 $/line	0.1% %/day	0.1% %/day	$10,000 $/accident
Annual Savings	*$750,000*	*$283,910*	*$260,000*	*$291,600*	*$120,000*	*$60,000*	*$40,000*
Total Savings ($s/year)	$1,805,510						
Payback Period (Years)	1.5						
Justifiable Investment	$2,708,265						

LOGISTICS RESOURCES
INTERNATIONAL, INC.

The value in the gap analysis is the single-page, graphical presentation of the performance profile. The analysis quickly points out weak and strong points in the performance of the operation. The gap chart can also be used to establish project goals. For example, in the figure, the inner ring may represent the current performance of an operation. Another ring may represent the goals of a reengineering project. The goal ring should be at or near world-class performance. If the goals of a project are not set high enough, because the definition of world-class performance is improving over time, at the completion of the project, the operation will not be improved relative to world-class performance.

Another use for the gap chart is in comparing operations in a potential benchmarking partnership. For the partnership to work effectively, the partners should not have overlapping, but offsetting strengths and weaknesses. If the strengths and weaknesses overlap, little learning can take place.

Finally, the gap analysis can also be used in justifying capital expenditures for new information and/or material handling systems. Because the chart quantifies the gap relative to world-class metrics, we can compute the annual monetary benefit (cost savings, cost avoidance, and/or revenue increases) of closing the gap in each performance area. The estimated annual benefit in relation to corporate payback goals suggests an appropriate investment available to close the gap.

The value of the analysis is heavily dependent on the validity of the outer ring. To help operators define these world-class targets, Logistics Resources International has developed a database of world-class warehouse performance indicators for a variety of industries.

3.4 WAREHOUSE PERFORMANCE INDEX

Do you think it would be possible to combine all those performance indicators into a single performance assessment for a warehouse? Another professor and I thought you could. In fact, Dr. Steve Hackman and I worked for two years to combine the performance indicators described previously into a single warehouse performance indicator, the *warehouse performance index* (WPI). The development of the index and related warehouse design and management conclusions are described in this section.

The WPI is developed with a utility theory technique called *data envelope analysis*. The technique is used to compute a productivity index from a series of mission outputs (such as orders shipped, material stored, and receipts processed) and resource consumptions (such as labor hours, square footage, and systems investment). An example is provided in Figure 3-4.

FIGURE 3-4   **Data envelope analysis graph.**
Source: Frazelle and Hackman, Warehouse Performance Index, The Logistics Institute, Georgia Institute of Technology.

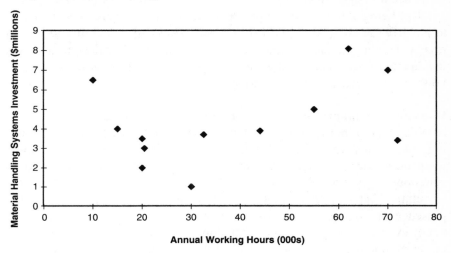

Imagine the points on the graph represent warehouses that shipped an identical amount and mix of product last year. Each operation has different values of labor hours consumed and different values of mechanization investment. The operations closest to the origin are the best performers— achieving the same output with fewer resources. The mathematical technique computes the distance of each point from the origin. The operation closest to the origin receives a perfect score of 100. The scores of the other operations are determined based on their distance from the origin relative to the operation with a perfect score.

This example in two dimensions of resource consumption and one dimension of output is presented to introduce the technique. The DEA methodology enables a multiplicity of resources and a multiplicity of outputs. In our research, we explored a wide variety of resource-output models for warehouse operations. The most reliable model centered on the consumption of the three major warehousing resources—labor, space, and material handling systems—used in achieving the mission of the warehouse —perfect shipping and storing inventory. However, because labor is the dominant factor in the resource model, and shipping activity is the dominant factor in the output model, the overall results correlate closely (not perfectly) with warehouse workforce productivity. Although this technique is not precise enough to distinguish between fine lines of performance (that is, between 85 and 87), our experience in sharing the results with a number of companies suggests that the technique is adequate for overall warehouse performance assessments (that is, excellent, good, average, or poor).

Just being able to assign a performance score to a warehouse is useful to identify the application of best practices. However, the ability to in turn review the performance scores and their relation with key design factors is invaluable for insights into the application and integration of the key warehouse resources: labor, space, and systems.

Workforce Demographics and Warehouse Performance

A wide range of human resource data was collected at each facility, including wage rates, the number of direct and indirect positions and hours involved in each warehousing function, the average education achieved by warehouse operators, and union composition. Of particular interest was the correlation between the computed warehouse performance index and the presence or absence of unions. Interestingly, our observations are split nearly evenly between union and nonunion operations. Would you expect that union or nonunion operations would have a higher average performance score?

The average performance index for union facilities was nearly identical to that of the nonunion facilities. In reviewing our observation and interview notes, we observed that union operations that exhibited high performance all made strategic use of management tactics to automatically pace the flow of work. Those tactics included

- Time standards and incentives to motivate high productivity
- Radio frequency terminals and light-directed picking to establish continuous, real-time monitoring of transactions
- Automated material handling systems to machine-pace the work flow and facilitate supervision

Ford and Chrysler Service Parts   At Ford and Chrysler, all of these techniques have been combined at their service parts distribution centers. All of their U.S. service parts distribution centers have been reconfigured around carousel-driven, light-directed order picking. In each operation, an order picker is assigned to a pod of three horizontal carousels: left, center, and right. While the order picker is picking from one carousel, the other two carousels are rotating to the next pick location. As a result, the order picker is never traveling and never idle waiting on a carousel. A vertical light display in front of each carousel indicates and directs the order picker to pick the correct quantity from the correct location. With parts in hand, the order picker turns to sort the parts into customer order totes. The totes are in light-directed flow rack located directly behind the operator. The correct sortation of the parts into customer order totes is directed by a horizontal light display on the flow rack.

In this operating scenario, the carousels eliminate traveling, help to pace the work, and facilitate supervision because all the operators should be aligned at their order picking stations. The picking and sortation lights also help to pace the flow of work and provide transaction times for operator productivity tracking. Time standards and incentives, based on productivity tracking data provided by the light-directed systems, also serve to increase productivity.

In retrospect, these management techniques all have something in common; they automate and facilitate the supervision of the workforce—one of the keys to effectively managing a union or any workforce.

Warehouse Size and Warehouse Performance

Do you think large or small warehouses tend to have better performance?

A variety of data points was used to assess the scale of each warehouse operation, including annual throughput, number of items housed in the warehouse, number of shipping and receiving docks, annual sales, and total floorspace measured in square footage. In no case were we able to make a definitive statement concerning the quantifiable relationship between the scale of warehouse operations and warehouse performance. However, based on the results displayed in Figure 3-5, there appears to be very little support

FIGURE 3-5   Warehouse performance index versus warehouse size.
Source: Frazelle and Hackman, Warehouse Performance Index, The Logistics Institute, Georgia Institute of Technology.

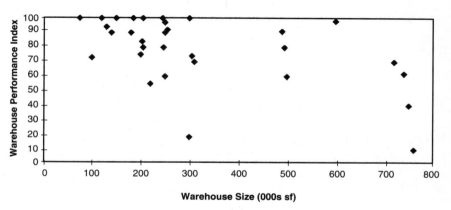

for the theory of strong economies of scale in warehousing and distribution operations.

In large facilities, the inherent productivity hurdles of excessive travel distances, poor work flow visibility, and difficult communication and supervision appear to offset any economies brought on by increased order volumes or high levels of mechanization. In large facilities, the travel time penalties for improper slotting, order batching, or task sequencing seem to grow exponentially with the size of facility. For example, in one 2 million square foot distribution center, the productivity penalties for improper slotting, batching, and sequencing result in an annual walking budget for the warehouse of over $3 million.

The size of the warehouse also tends to increase the span of control. The greater the span of control, the more skilled the managers and supervisors need to be. Unfortunately, there is a severe shortage in the number of highly skilled warehouse operations managers and supervisors. As a result, as a warehouse grows, the management requirements can quickly exceed the management and supervisory capability.

The Level of Mechanization and Warehouse Performance

Are highly mechanized operations more productive than conventional warehouses?

Based on our analysis and confirmed in a variety of project settings, we cannot assume that a high degree of mechanization will yield a high warehouse performance (see Figure 3-6). In fact, a high degree of mechanization may yield just the opposite effect. How could that happen? Excess complexity, inadequate or no training, ill-advised experimentation, subjective decision making, improper financial justification, and inflexibility are just some of the ways.

3.5   DO'S AND DON'TS FOR WAREHOUSE AUTOMATION

This list of do's and don'ts will help you avoid some of the traps of warehouse automation and mechanization.

Don't assume automation can resolve a complex situation. *Do* simplify first.

We often believe automation is a way to streamline a complex process, manage a complex process, and/or make a complex process more efficient. Instead, automation is inherently complex. By applying complexity to a complex situation, we get complexity squared. The correct approach is to simplify and streamline a process first—taking as much work content out as possible. At that point, there may not be enough work content left to auto-

FIGURE 3-6 **Warehouse performance index versus level of mechanization.**
Source: Frazelle and Hackman, Warehouse Performance Index, The Logistics Institute, Georgia Institute of Technology.

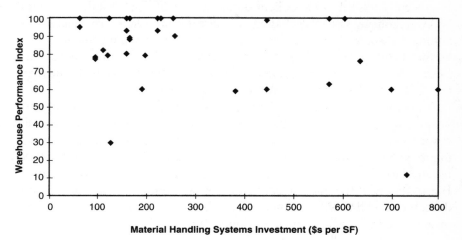

mate, and/or what remains will be simple and consistent enough to reliably automate. Automation should not be the first, but rather the last resort.

It is human nature (or what has evolved to become human nature since the dawning of sales people) to believe that machines can solve problems. A classic example is the NordicTrack. Suppose I need to lose 10 pounds (which I do). There I am sitting on the sofa in front of the TV eating potato chips. Guess what commercial comes on? You guessed right, the NordicTrack commercial with super-fit models gliding along and losing pounds right there in front of my eyes. The 1-800 number comes on the screen. All I need is a credit card. Voila! I am 10 pounds lighter—in my dreams. In fact, if it was that easy, I would lose the 10 pounds when they debited my credit card.

Unfortunately, it doesn't work that way. I have to assemble the machine, read the instructions, and worse yet, follow a regimented program of disciplined exercise and performance monitoring. Even worse, I have to diet and keep track of my eating to make all this work. All of a sudden, I have discovered the truth.

What makes a difference is my behavior and disciplines, not the machine. In fact, the machine is only a tool. If I do not use it properly, it will not be helpful and may even cause injury. Get the point? The situation is the same with a carousel, new order picker truck, new warehouse management system, or any other new system.

Don't take training and documentation for granted. *Do* appropriate the necessary training and documentation time and budget.

We recently worked with a client on the west coast that installed a $3 million warehousing system including light directed carousels, wave picking and automated sortation, and a supporting warehouse management system. Unfortunately, all of the WKPIs—productivity, accuracy, and response time —are worse now than they were before the system was installed. The major reason for the system failure is the absence of any training or system documentation. In the heated bidding competition, the low bidder secured the position by removing training and documentation from its proposal, and they never made its way back in. Now, would you as the project champion be willing to go back to the board of directors and ask for the additional $300,000 required to train the affected people and document the systems? I hope so. But in this instance, the project champion will not take that step. Until he does, the company will continue to own and operate a Mazzerati without an owner's manual and without a driving course.

Don't be the Guinea Pig. *Do* see and evaluate the proposed system in a live setting.

I recently took a call from the head legal counsel for a large snack foods company. The counsel indicated that his company wanted to bring a lawsuit against a material handling supplier whose wire-guided order picker trucks would not run in reverse. They wanted to bring a lawsuit to reclaim productivity damages.

As usual, I started to ask questions about the circumstances surrounding the case. First, I asked if the design team had ever seen this sort of system in operation. Counsel indicated they had. Next, I asked where they had seen it. Counsel indicated that the team visited one of the beta-site installations. Unfortunately, the system was not operating that day, but they had seen a video where the system was really working well. What can I say? Next case!

Don't justify and design the system in a vacuum. *Do* use a cross-functional team including, operations, engineering, customer service, and systems on the team.

I was involved in a recent project in which the project team was dominated by a boisterous former military logistician. He quickly became known as Captain Carousels because no matter what the analysis indicated, no matter what the wishes of the group were, no matter, no matter, no matter, according to him, we were going to have carousels in his warehouse. Whether convinced by a clever sales person, captivated by an advertisement and/or case study in a magazine, or whether from past experience, Captain Carousels was one big obstacle that had to be overcome. If he was allowed to act independently, you can only imagine the outcome. Unfortunately, it happens.

One of my business partners always says that, "People will only successfully implement what they design themselves." It is true. If the cross-functional team designs the solution, then for their own self-preservation, they will make it work.

> *Don't* accept the justification of the new system relative to the existing situation. *Do* incrementally justify the project relative to an improved current situation.

Imagine that a material handling or warehouse management system's supplier brings a project to you that costs $1 million and can yield $1 million in annual cost savings. The one year payback seems attractive. All systems go, right? Wrong. In this case, the $1 million in annual savings is the yield relative to the current, lousy situation. Many millions of capital dollars have been justified against a current lousy situation. The correct approach is to consider the investment relative to the current situation modified by very inexpensive process improvements. Then the improved state becomes the right backdrop against which to consider the large initial investment. For example, in warehousing, many of the WKPIs can be improved through improved slotting, order batching, picking tour construction, and work flow simplification. These improvements typically yield a 20 to 30 percent improvement in overall warehouse productivity, yet they can be realized with a small initial investment. After these improvements have been made, a large investment can be considered. However, in the case of the $1 million, we were considering relative to a $1 million annual savings, the remaining annual savings may only be $250,000. In that case, the payback period is four years. That may or may not be justifiable. Either way, it is the correct financial assessment, and the process improvements that were made will increase the likelihood of success for the investment project. This approach to project justification is called incremental justification (see Figure 3-7).

Admittedly, there are situations when a capital investment is made solely with infrastructure, competitive, and/or customer service justifications. In those cases, the project should be labeled and audited as such.

> *Don't* assume a higher level of mechanization will bring increased flexibility. *Do* consider that higher levels of mechanization bring flexibility risk.

FIGURE 3-7   **Incremental justification approach.**

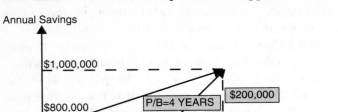

Highly mechanized systems are typically difficult to reconfigure. For example, a consumer electronics company recently designed, purchased, and installed an automated storage and retrieval system for pallet handling. Six months after the system was installed, the order patterns changed dramatically, requiring case as opposed to pallet quantity customer shipments. Because the pallet handling system was not conducive to case picking, and because the highly automated system was nearly impossible to reconfigure, the company was forced to either suffer the productivity penalty in working around the new system or initiate the design of an entirely new system.

3.6 WAREHOUSE PRACTICES AND WAREHOUSE PERFORMANCE

After presenting all of this analysis, I am often asked what separates world-class performers from the rest of the pack. Well, after all is said and done, the major distinguishing feature of world-class performing warehouses is their practices. You often hear basketball or football coaches say that their team performs the way they practice. It is the same in warehousing. The warehouse performs as a function of its practices. In other words, the performance indicators, good or bad, are a direct result of the design and management of the underlying processes in the warehouse. We often look for excuses such as a lack of resources, the burden of the union, the attitude of the executives, and so on. The bottom line is the processes, polices, and procedures that are carried out inside the four walls of the warehouse.

To help people evaluate their warehousing practices, I developed a warehouse practices gap analysis similar in concept to the warehouse performance gap analysis. The major difference is that practice descriptions are not quantifiable. Instead, for each functional area in the warehouse (receiving, putaway, storage, replenishment, slotting, order picking, shipping, communications, and work measurement), I describe world-class (stage 5), middle-class (stage 3), and no-class (stage 1) practices (see Figure 3-8).

For example, no-class receiving would proceed as follows: When a receipt shows up, we have no idea it is coming. We have no idea what is in the receipt and if and/or when we ordered it. Because we had no idea the receipt was coming, there is no crew available to unload the truck and potentially no dock available. When a crew and/or dock is available, we open the door, unload the receipt, and stage it at the dock.

Finally, we have somebody pull some paperwork on the receipt, match it with a purchase order, and correct the purchase orders (assuming the receipts we found are right). Then, we ask a lift truck operator to put the loads away, one at a time, finding the nearest open location or aisle for the loads and memorizing the putaway location(s). It is getting a little ridiculous, right? Unfortunately, this ridiculous example hits very close to home for some operators.

FIGURE 3-8   World-Class Warehousing Practices

PROCESS	Stage 1	Stage 2	Stage 3	Stage 4	Stage 5
Receiving	Unload, stage, & in-check	Immediate putaway to reserve	Immediate putaway to primary	Cross-docking	Prereceiving
Putaway	First-come-first-serve	Batched by zone	Batched & sequenced	Location-to-stocker	Automated putaway
Reserve Storage	Floor storage	Conventional racking & bins	Some double deep storage	Some narrow aisle storage	Optimal hybrid storage
Picking	Pick-to-single-order	Batch picking	Zone picking—Progressive assembly	Zone picking—Downstream sorting	Dynamic picking
Slotting	Random	Popularity based	Popularity and cube based	Popularity, cube, and correlation based	Dynamic slotting
Replenishment	As needed—Pick face complete	As needed—Downstream complete	Anticipated—By sight	Anticipated—Automated	Pick from reserve storage
Shipping	Check, stage, & load	Stage & load	Direct load	Automated loading	Pick-to-trailer
Work Measurement	No standards	Standards used for planning	Standards used for evaluation	Standards used for incentive pay	Standards used for continuous feedback
Communications	Paper	Bar code scanning	RF terminals	Handsfree	Virtual displays

Burlington Industries   Now, to stage 5, world-class receiving. At Burlington Industries, pallet loads coming off of manufacturing lines are loaded
directly onto outbound trailers for shipping. Each pallet has a bar coded
license plate, which a lift truck operator scans as he picks the load up at the
end of the manufacturing line. As the lift truck operator takes the load onto
the outbound trailer, he scans a bar code label above the shipping door to
log the load onto the outbound load. When all the loads have been positioned
on the trailer, the load is closed out and an *advance shipping notice* (ASN)
is forwarded to the customer indicating the time the load is leaving, the exact
position of each pallet on the truck, and the scheduled arrival time.

In addition, each outbound trailer has a RF tag embedded in the windshield. As the truck makes its way toward the customer location, antennas
located every 10 miles along the highway read the tag as the truck goes by
to update the customer's system as to the location and expected arrival time.
Because the receipt was scheduled by the customer, a dock door and crew
are preassigned to the load. As each pallet is unloaded at the dock, the license
plate is scanned for an inquiry on the disposition of the load. The first check
is for cross-docking. If the item is required for an outstanding order, the lift
truck operator is directed to take the load to the trailer where that load is
being prepared. Otherwise, the lift truck operator is directed to a preassigned
location (assigned by the warehouse management system during the in-
transit time) for the item. The first choice is a primary pick location if it
needs restocking, then the reserve location.

Now, compare the amount of material handling and elapsed time in each
example. The key to improving warehouse performance is in reducing the
work content, primarily material and information handling. Every time a
piece of material or paper is handled, the amount of time and resources
required to do the job increases. Also, every time a piece of material or information is handled, the likelihood of error increases.

To help people benchmark their practices against world-class, I created
a methodology similar to warehouse performance gap analysis. As you may
have guessed, it is called warehouse practices gap analysis. An example is
illustrated in Figure 3-9. Each of the radials represent one of the functional
areas in the warehouse. As before, the outer ring defines world-class standards. The practices of the warehouse are then plotted relative to the world-
class definitions provided earlier. As before, this technique can be used to
set project goals, to assess benchmarking partners, and in this particular
example to conduct a functional evaluation of a warehouse management
system.

FIGURE 3-9   Warehouse practices gap analysis.

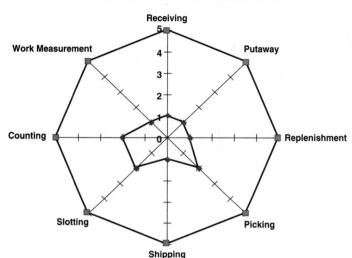

3.7   SUMMARY

- Benchmarking is a critical step on the way to world-class warehousing.

- External benchmarking should be used to set world-class goals for the warehouse operations and process improvement projects.

- The benchmarking process should jointly consider all the major warehouse performance indicators including, productivity, shipping accuracy, inventory accuracy, dock-to-stock time, warehouse order cycle time, and the level of mechanization.

- Benchmarking and warehouse performance gap analysis should be used to incrementally justify capital expenditures.

- Benchmarking and warehouse practices analysis should be used to align the warehouse practices with world-class standards.

S E C T I O N

INNOVATING WAREHOUSE OPERATIONS

C H A P T E R

4

RECEIVING AND PUTAWAY PRINCIPLES

W
HAT IS THE HIGHEST WAREHOUSING productivity possible? One hundred lines per person-hour? No, I have seen operations where the warehousing productivity is more than 2,000 lines per person-hour. Is that the highest? No. In fact, there can be infinite productivity in the warehouse. Recall the definition of labor productivity. The numerator is the output, lines or units picked; the denominator is the input, person-hours. This ratio could be infinity if the denominator goes to zero. In other words, if we could somehow get the warehousing work done without having anyone employed in the warehouse, then we could achieve infinite warehousing productivity.

Sounds great. Is it possible? Absolutely. There are two possibilities. The first is to completely automate the warehouse. Believe it or not, there are large case picking operations in Japan in which no human touches a pallet or a case, from receiving to shipping. In Germany, there are broken case picking operations in which no human touches the product. In these operations, the warehousing picking productivity is indeed infinity. Unfortunately, the investment required is nearly infinity as well. Better than completely automating the warehouse is to completely eliminate the need for it via direct shipping or minimize the need for it via cross-docking. When those practices cannot be employed, we will need to consider the options for simplifying and streamlining the traditional receiving and putaway activities.

4.1   RECEIVING

Receiving is the setup for all other warehousing activities. If we don't receive merchandise properly it will be very difficult to handle it properly in putaway, storage, picking, or shipping. If we allow damaged or inaccurate deliveries in the door, we are likely to ship damaged or inaccurate shipments out the door.

The world-class receiving principles presented here are meant to serve as guidelines for streamlining receiving operations. They are intended to simplify the flow of material through the receiving process and to insure the minimum work content is required. Minimizing work content, mistakes, time, and accidents is accomplished in logistics by reducing handling steps. Figure 4-1 illustrates the reduction in handling steps that can be achieved by applying advanced receiving and putaway practices.

The following world-class receiving practices are described and illustrated in the following:

- Direct shipping
- Cross-docking
- Receiving scheduling
- Prereceiving
- Receipt preparation

Direct Shipping
For some materials, the best receiving is no receiving. In direct (or drop) shipping, vendors bypass our warehouse completely and ship directly to the

FIGURE 4-1   Touch analysis for alternative receiving practices.

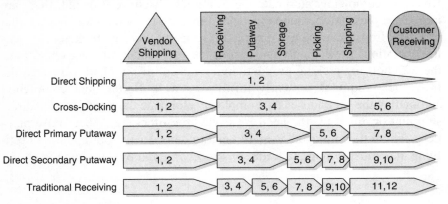

customer. Because the items never arrive at the DC, they do not have to be unloaded, staged, put away, replenished to a forward pick location, picked, packed, checked, staged, and loaded. Hence, all the labor, time, and equipment normally consumed and all the mistakes and accidents that often occur in the warehouse are eliminated.

Every justifiable direct shipment should be aggressively pursued. Opportunities for direct shipping include large, bulky items, made-to-order items, and combinations of items for which the regular shipping volume occupies at least a full truckload. For example, a large camping and sportswear mail order distributor drop ships all the canoes and large tents that are advertised in their catalog instead of shipping from their central DC. The food industry is also adopting more direct shipping. More and more food and consumer products manufacturers are making and assembling store orders at their factories for direct delivery to their retail customers' store locations.

Cross-Docking

When material cannot be shipped direct, the next best option may be cross-docking. In cross-docking

- Loads are scheduled for delivery into the warehouse from vendors
- Inbound materials are sorted immediately into their outbound orders
- Outbound orders are transported immediately to their outbound dock
- Receiving staging or inspection is not required
- Product storage is not required.

In so doing, the traditional warehousing activities involving receiving inspection, receiving staging, putaway, storage, pick location replenishment, order picking, and order assembly are eliminated.

Certain containerization and communication requirements must be met before high-volume cross-docking can be implemented. First, each container and product must be automatically identifiable through a bar code label or RF tag. Second, loads must be scheduled into the DC and assigned to dock doors automatically. Third, inbound pallets or cases that will be cross-docked should contain only a single SKU or be preconfigured for their destination to minimize sortation requirements.

In addition to normal order flows, backorders, special orders, and transfer orders are good candidates for cross-docking because the sense of urgency to process those orders is high, the inbound merchandise is prepackaged and labeled for delivery to the ultimate customer, and the merchandise on those orders does not have to be merged with other merchandise to complete a customers requirements.

Cross-Docking the Amway Way Amway is a major manufacturer and direct-to-consumer distributor of consumer and personal products including soaps, cleaning supplies, and cosmetics. At its central distribution center in Ada, Michigan, receipts from manufacturing are scheduled and all incoming pallets have bar code license plates (see Figure 4-2). As a lift truck operator unloads a trailer, a pallet license plate (bar code) is scanned to inform the warehouse management system that the pallet is on site. The warehouse management system then directs the operator to move the inbound pallet to its assigned warehouse location. The first priority for the pallet is cross-docking. In fact, if the item is required in an outstanding order that is currently being loaded (and if there is no violation of code-date expiration windows for pallets in inventory of the same item), the operator is directed to move (cross-dock) the pallet to that dock for shipping. The next priority is *direct-putaway* to a primary pick location. This transaction is recommended if there is an opening for the pallet in the primary pick location. The last priority is to move the pallet to its reserve warehouse location. Even in that case, there is no stag-

FIGURE 4-2 **Receiving flows concept plan.**
Source: James M. Apple, Jr.

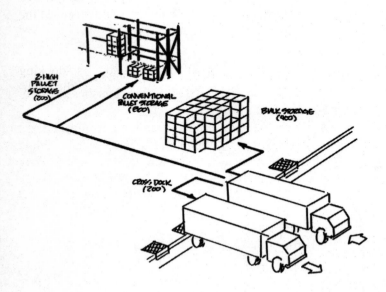

ing of the product because locations are either preassigned or assigned in real-time. (Some warehouses are purposefully designed without receiving staging space to discourage any receiving staging.)

K-Mart Cross-Docking   At K-Mart's jewelry distribution center, suppliers are required to bar code license plate each carton. At the receiving dock, inbound cartons are properly oriented and manually off-loaded onto a telescoping conveyor. The telescoping conveyor feeds a sortation conveyor just inside the doors of the DC. A bar code scanner located on the conveyor reads the carton license plate to make the real-time warehouse management system aware that the carton is on site. In turn, the warehouse management system instructs the conveyor to direct the carton to the cross-docking operation (if there is an outstanding open order for the item) or to the traditional store, pick, pack, and ship operation otherwise.

In the cross-docking operation, each K-Mart store has a tote position in one of six carousels. As an inbound carton is presented to a carousel operator, the operator is directed by a CRT and a light tree to distribute the contents of the carton to the stores in the carousel carrier in front of the operator. The contents of the carton are depleted this way. When a store order is complete, a flashing light display indicates that the corresponding order is complete. The operator pushes the tote through the back of the carousel where a takeaway conveyor takes the tote to shipping. More than 50 percent of the merchandise in the DC is cross-docked in this manner.

Cross-Docking in the Food Industry   Direct shipping and cross-docking are so effective that entire industries are taking steps to maximize the application of these principles. For example, the logistics of *efficient consumer response* (ECR) makes direct shipping and cross-docking the foundation of physical distribution in the grocery industry. A classic example is from a $2 billion grocer headquartered in Grand Rapids, Michigan (see Figure 4-3). There, the A movers (based on cube-movement) are shipped in truckload quantities from food manufacturers to grocery retail stores. B movers are precisely scheduled into a central DC for daily cross-docking to build consolidated (frozen, refrigerated, and ambient temperature) loads for retail stores. C movers are stored in a contiguous DC specially designed for dense storage and batch picking of slow moving items. A daily batch is picked of the C items and inducted into the cross-docking operation. (Of course, to take advantage of this operating philosophy, the warehouse activity profiling is critical and must be done continuously.)

FIGURE 4-3   Supply chain flows in the food industry.
Source: Bruce A. Strahan

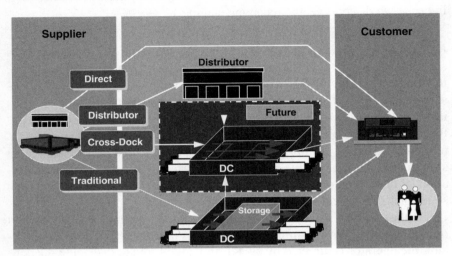

Receiving Scheduling

True, premeditated cross-docking requires the ability to schedule inbound loads to match outbound requirements on a daily or even hourly basis. In addition, balancing the use of receiving resources—dock doors, personnel, staging space, and material handling equipment—requires the ability to schedule carriers and to shift time consuming receipts to offpeak hours. Through the Internet, EDI, and/or fax links, companies have improved access to schedule information on inbound and outbound loads. This information can and should be used to proactively schedule receipts and to provide *advance shipping notice* (ASN) information.

Prereceiving

The rationale for staging at the receiving dock, the most time and space intensive activity in the receiving function, is often the need to hold material for location assignment, product identification, and so on. This information can often be captured ahead of time by having the information communicated by the vendor at the time of shipment via the Internet, EDI link, or via fax notification. In some cases, the information describing an inbound load can be captured on a smart card, enabling immediate input of the information at the receiving dock. Load contents can also be communi-

FIGURE 4-4   Optical memory card.
Source: U.S. Army Logistics Command

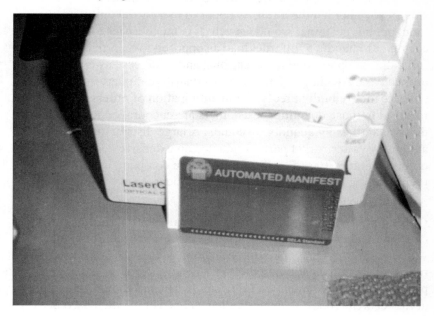

cated in RF tags readable by antennae located along major highways, at each receiving dock, on lift trucks, and/or conveyors.

Figure 4-4 depicts an optical memory card used to download the contents of an entire trailer load into a PC at a receiving dock.

Receipt Preparation

The most time we ever have available to prepare a product for shipment is at the moment it is received. Once the demand for a product has been received, there is precious little time available for additional preparation of the product prior to shipment. Hence, any material processing that can be accomplished ahead of time should be accomplished. Those preparatory activities include

- **Prepackaging in issue increments**   If there are 100 cartons on a pallet, and a customer orders 100 cartons, would you rather pick a full pallet, or handle 100 individual cartons? You did not need to buy this book to learn that it requires much less time and work to handle the full pallet. The same could be said for a full case as opposed to breaking a case open for order picking, or for a full truckload container as opposed to loose pallets on a LTL shipment. Not only would we rather handle a full, as opposed to a partial unit load at a time, but our customer would as well. It is much easier for our customer to handle a full truckload as opposed to a partial truckload, a full pallet as opposed to loose cartons, and a full case as opposed to a broken case. At a large office supplies distributor, quarter- and half-pallet loads are built at receiving in anticipation of orders being received in those quantities. Customers are encouraged to order in those quantities by quantity discounts. A large distributor of automotive aftermarket parts conducted an extensive analysis of likely order quantities. Based on that analysis, the company is now prepackaging in those popular issue increments.

- **Applying necessary labels and tags**
- **Cubing and weighing for storage and transport planning**   Product cube and weight information is used to make a myriad of key warehouse design and operating decisions, yet few organizations have reliable cube information on their products. If suppliers cannot provide product cube and weight, the information can and should be captured at the receiving dock. A device called a *cubiscan* is often used at receiving to capture and automatically communicate inbound carton dimensions and weights (see Figure 4-5).

4.2   PUTAWAY
Putaway is order picking in reverse. Many of the principles that streamline the picking process work well for putaway. In order, the world-class principles for putaway are

- Direct putaway
- Directed putaway
- Batched and sequenced putaway
- Interleaving

Direct Putaway
   Putaway directly to primary or reserve locations.

One of our large healthcare clients does not allow staging space to be included in their warehouse layouts. They want to force warehouse operators to put goods away immediately upon receipt as opposed to the delays and multiple handlings that are characteristic of traditional receiving and putaway activities.

FIGURE 4-5   Automatic cubing and weighing.

When material cannot be cross-docked, material handling steps can be minimized by bypassing receiving staging and putting material away directly to primary picking locations, essentially replenishing primary locations from the receiving dock. When there are no severe constraints on product rotation, this may be feasible. Otherwise, material should be directly put-away to reserve locations.

In direct putaway systems, staging and inspection activities are eliminated. Hence, the time, space, and labor associated with those operations is eliminated.

Vehicles that serve the dual purpose of truck unloading and product putaway facilitate direct putaway. For example, counterbalanced lift trucks can be equipped with scales, cubing devices, and online RF terminals to streamline the unloading and putaway function.

The world's most advanced logistics operations are characterized by automated, direct putaway to storage locations. The material handling technologies that facilitate direct putaway include roller-bed trailers and extendable conveyors (see Figure 4-6). (The prequalification of vendors to support direct putaway and prereceiving is described in Chapter 6, "Case Picking Systems.")

FIGURE 4-6   Automated, direct putaway.

Directed Putaway

Left to their own devices, most putaway operators naturally choose putaway locations that are easiest to locate, nearest the floor, nearest their friend, nearest the break room, using any criteria except where the putaway should be located to maximize storage density and operating productivity. The *warehouse management system* (WMS) should direct the putaway operators to place each pallet or case in the location that maximizes location and cube utilization, insures good product rotation, and maximizes retrieval productivity (see Figure 4-7).

Batched and Sequenced Putaway

Sort inbound materials for efficient putaway.

Just as zone picking and location sequencing are effective strategies for improving order picking productivity, inbound materials can and should be sorted for putaway by warehouse zone and by location sequence.

Figure 4-8 illustrates an example of putaway batching at a large Dutch shoe distributor. All shoes that will be put away in the same aisle are sorted

FIGURE 4-7   RF directed putaway operation.

FIGURE 4-8   Batched and sequenced putaways.

FIGURE 4-9   Interleaving concept.

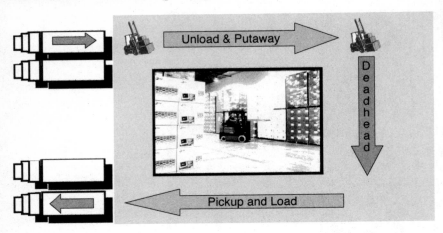

down a particular conveyor lane and stacked in putaway location sequence automatically.

Interleaving and Continuous Moves

Combine putaways and retrievals when possible.

To further streamline the putaway and retrieval process, putaway and retrieval transactions can be combined in a dual command to reduce the amount of empty travel (deadheading) by lift trucks (see Figure 4-9). This technique is especially geared for pallet storage and retrieval operations. Counterbalance lift trucks that can unload, putaway, retrieve, and load are an efficient means for executing dual commands. (Interleaving is similar to backhauling in transportation.) The practice of interleaving should be extended to continuous moves within the warehouse, where warehouse operators are directed from most-efficient-task to most-efficient-task by the WMS.

5

PALLET STORAGE AND RETRIEVAL SYSTEMS

O UR DESCRIPTION OF PALLET storage and retrieval systems is organized into two sections—pallet storage systems and pallet retrieval systems. Though the decisions are interdependent, the storage system selection is driven primarily by the concern for improved storage density and is dictated by the on-hand inventory and turnover of the items in pallet storage (Section 5.1, "Pallet Storage Operations"). The retrieval system selection is driven primarily by the concern for high handling productivity and tradeoffs in required capital investment (Section 5.2, "Pallet Retrieval Operations"). We close this chapter with a case study comparison of alternative pallet storage and handling methods (Section 5.3, "Pallet Storage/Retrieval Systems Selection").

5.1 PALLET STORAGE SYSTEMS

The most popular pallet storage systems are

- Block stacking
- Stacking frames
- Single-deep selective pallet rack
- Double-deep rack
- Drive-in rack
- Drive-thru rack

- Pallet flow rack
- Push-back rack

Each alternative—its pros, cons, and related costs—is described in the following sections.

Block Stacking

Block stacking (see Figure 5-1) refers to unit loads stacked on top of each other and stored on the floor in storage lanes (blocks), two to ten loads deep. Depending on the weight and stability of the loads, stacks may range from two loads high to a height determined by

- Acceptable safe limits
- Load stackability
- Load weights
- Pallet conditions
- Floor loading restrictions
- Weather (due to corrugated softening in high humidity)
- Vehicle lift height capacity
- Crushability of the loads
- Building clear height

FIGURE 5-1   Block stacking.

FIGURE 5-2   Block stacking layout.
Source: Naval Supply Systems Command

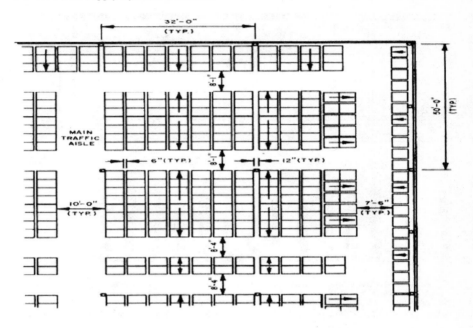

Loads in a block (see Figure 5-2) should be retrieved under a *last-in-first-out* (LIFO) discipline. Hence, if highly restrictive (more strict than lot or code date) FIFO requirements are in place, block stacking is not a feasible storage method. Block stacking is particularly effective when there are multiple pallets per *stock keeping unit* (SKU) and when inventory is turned in large increments, that is, several loads of the same SKU are received or withdrawn at one time.

As loads are removed from a storage lane, a space-loss phenomenon referred to as *honeycombing* occurs with block stacking. Because only one SKU can be effectively stored in a lane, empty pallet spaces are created that cannot be utilized effectively until an entire lane is emptied. Therefore, in order to maintain high utilization of the available storage positions, the lane depth (number of loads stored from the aisle) must be carefully determined.

A lane depth optimization analysis developed for a recent client is presented in Figure 5-3. The lane depth yielding the lowest floorspace requirement for each item is recommended through the analysis.

FIGURE 5-3   **Lane depth optimization.**
Source: LRI Slotting Optimization

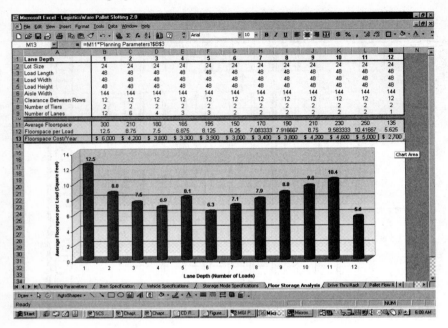

An estimate of the optimal lane depth can be calculated from the following formula:

$$\text{Optimal lane depth} = [(\text{Aisle width} \times \text{Lot size})/(2 \times \text{Load length} \times \text{Stack height})]^{1/2}$$

Because no racking is required, the investment in a block stacking system is low, block stacking is easy to implement, and it enables near-infinite flexibility for floorspace configuration.

Pallet Stacking Frames

Pallet stacking frames (see Figure 5-4) are either frames attached to standard wooden pallets or self-contained steel units made up of decks and posts. Stacking frames are portable and enable the user to stack material several loads high. When not in use, the frames can be disassembled and stored in a minimum amount of space.

Stacking frames are commonly used when loads are not stackable and when other racking alternatives are not justifiable. Also, because stacking

FIGURE 5-4   Pallet stacking frame.

frames can be leased, they are popular when there is a short-term spike in inventory and the frames are needed to increase storage density in what is normally open floorspace.

A single stacking frame costs between $100 and $300. The storage density losses due to honeycombing described earlier for block stacking also apply to stacking frames.

Single-Deep Pallet Rack

Single-deep pallet racking (see Figure 5-5) is a simple construction of metal uprights and cross-members providing immediate (pick-face) access to each load stored (that is, no honeycombing). Unlike block stacking, when a pallet space is created by the removal of a load, a pallet opening is immediately available in single-deep racking. Also, because racking supports every load, stacking height is not limited by the stackability and/or crushability of the loads, and multiple SKUs can be stacked in the same vertical column of storage space.

Loads do not need to be stackable and may be of varying heights and widths. In instances where the load depth is highly variable, it may be necessary to provide load supports or decking.

FIGURE 5-5 Single-deep pallet rack.

A typical single-deep rack position costs between $40 and $50. The major advantage is full accessibility to all unit loads. The major disadvantage is the amount of space devoted to aisles—typically 50 to 60 percent of the available floor space. As a result, in cases where there are three or more pallets on-hand of a SKU, a storage method that houses at least two pallets in a facing perpendicular to the storage aisle is preferable.

Selective pallet rack might be considered the *benchmark* storage mode, against which other systems may be compared for advantages and disadvantages. Most storage systems benefit from the use of at least some selective pallet rack for SKUs whose storage requirement is less than three to five pallet loads.

Double-Deep Pallet Rack

Double-deep pallet racks (see Figure 5-6) are merely selective racks that are two pallet positions deep. The advantage of two-deep rack facings (perpendicular to the aisle) is that fewer aisles are needed. In most cases, a 50 percent aisle space savings is achieved versus single-deep selective rack. However, we cannot assume that a 50 percent true space savings will be achieved because we can only anticipate a 70 to 75 percent utilization of the

FIGURE 5-6   **Double-deep pallet rack.**
Source: Crown

available openings (due to honeycombing). (80 to 85 percent utilization is common for single deep racking.)

Double-deep racks are typically used when the storage requirement for a SKU is five pallets or greater and when product is received and picked frequently in multiples of two pallets. (Assigning SKUs with only a single pallet on-hand to double-deep racking is nonsensical because one of the two positions in a facing is automatically wasted.) Because pallets are stored two deep, a double reach fork lift is required for storage/retrieval.

Drive-In Rack
Drive-in racks (see Figure 5-7) extend the reduction of aisle space begun with double-deep pallet rack by providing storage lanes from five to ten loads deep and three to five loads high. Drive-in racks enable a lift truck to drive into the rack several pallet positions and store or retrieve a pallet. This is

FIGURE 5-7   Drive-in and drive-thru rack.

possible because the rack consists of upright columns with horizontal rails to support pallets at a height above that of the lift truck. This construction yields multiple levels of pallet storage.

One drawback of drive-in rack is the reduction of lift truck travel speed needed for safe navigation within the confines of the rack construction. Another drawback is the honeycombing losses because no more than one SKU should be housed in a lane. As a result, drive-in rack is best used for slow to medium velocity SKUs with 20 or more pallets on-hand. As was the case with block stacking, loads should be retrieved with a LIFO discipline and with a retrieval discipline to free up each lane as quickly as possible.

Drive-Thru Rack

Drive-thru rack is merely drive-in rack that is accessible from both sides of the rack. It is for staging loads in a flow-thru fashion where a pallet is loaded at one end and retrieved at the other end. The same considerations for drive-in rack apply to drive-thru rack.

Pallet Flow Rack

Functionally, pallet flow rack (see Figure 5-8) is used like drive-thru rack. However, loads are conveyed (FIFO) on skate wheel conveyor, roller conveyor, or rails from one end of a storage lane to the other. As a load is

FIGURE 5-8   Pallet flow rack.
Source: Sure Flo

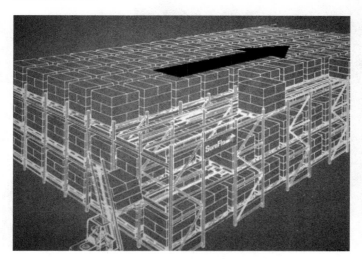

removed from the front of a storage lane, the next load advances to the pick face. The main purpose of pallet flow rack is to provide high throughput pallet storage and retrieval *and* good space utilization. Hence, it is used for those items with high pallet inventory turnover and with several pallets on-hand. The major disadvantage of pallet flow rack is the expense—$200 to $300 per storage position.

Push-Back Rack
Push-back rack (see Figure 5-9) provides last-in-first-out deep lane (two to five pallets deep) storage using a rail-guided carrier for each pallet load. As a load is placed into storage, its weight and the force of the putaway vehicle pushes the other loads in the lane back into the lane to create room for the additional load. As a load is removed from the front of a storage lane, the weight of the remaining load automatically advances remaining loads to the rack face. Hence, every SKU has a load that is immediately accessible. In addition, because all of the putaway and retrieval takes place at the rack face, there is no need for special lift truck attachments as was the case with double-deep rack. An advantage over drive-in rack is that there is no need to drive into the rack and there is no vertical honeycombing. Push-back rack is appropriate for medium to fast-moving SKUs with three to ten pallets on-hand. The cost of typical push-back rack is in the range of $150 per pallet position.

FIGURE 5-9   Push-back rack.

FIGURE 5-10   Mobile pallet rack.
Source: White

Mobile Pallet Rack

Mobile pallet racks (see Figure 5-10) are essentially single-deep pallet racks on wheels or tracks permitting an entire row of racks to move away from adjacent rack rows. The underlying principal is that aisles are only justified when they are being used; the rest of the time they are occupying valuable space. Access to a particular storage row is achieved by moving (mechanically or manually) the adjacent row and creating an aisle in front of the desired row. As a result, less than 10 percent of the floorspace is devoted to aisles, and storage density is the highest of any of the pallet storage alternatives. Unfortunately, the pallet storage retrieval productivity is the lowest of any of the alternatives we have considered. Hence, mobile racks are justifiable when space is scarce and expensive, and for slow-moving SKUs with one to three pallets on-hand. The cost of typical mobile rack is in the range of $250 per pallet position.

Pallet Storage Systems Selection
The key to selecting the appropriate pallet storage system configuration is to assign each SKU to a pallet storage system whose storage and productivity characteristics match the activity and inventory profile of the SKU. Table 5-1 and Figure 5-11 are designed to assist you in this matching process. Table 5-1 is a summary of the key features of each pallet storage system including cost, storage density, load accessibility, throughput capacity, inventory and location control, FIFO maintenance, load size variability, and ease of installation. The letters A, B, C, D, and F correspond to the evaluations of excellent, above average, average, below average, and poor.

Figure 5-11 illustrates an example pallet storage mode analysis. The example is taken from a particular case and cannot be generalized because the preference regions vary widely as a function of the cost and availability of labor and space. The analysis indicates the most economically appropriate assignment of popularity-inventory families to pallet storage modes.

5.2   PALLET RETRIEVAL SYSTEMS
The most popular pallet retrieval systems are

- Walkie stackers
- Counterbalance lift trucks
- Straddle trucks
- Straddle reach trucks
- Sideloader trucks
- Turret trucks
- Hybrid trucks
- *Automated storage and retrieval* (ASR) machines

TABLE 5-1 Pallet Storage Mode Selection and Evaluation Criteria

	Floor Storage	Stacking Frames	Single-Deep	Double-Deep	Drive-in Rack	Drive-Thru	Flow Rack	Push-Back	Mobile Rack	Cantilever
Cost per position	n/a	$50	$40	$50	$65	$65	$200	$150	$250	$80
Potential storage density	A	B	D	C	B	B	B	B	A	B
Load access	F	F	A	C	B	B	B	A	F	A
Throughput capacity	B	D	B	C	C	C	A	C	F	C
Inventory & location control	F	F	A	C	D	D	C	C	D	B
FIFO maintenance	F	F	A	C	D	D	A	C	C	A
Ability to house variable load sizes	A	D	C	C	D	D	F	C	C	B
Ease of installation	A	A	C	C	C	C	F	C	F	B

FIGURE 5-11   Example of pallet storage mode economic analysis.

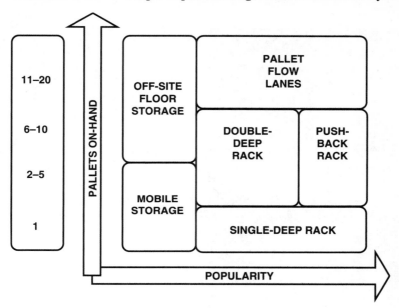

The applications, pros, cons, and related costs of each system are described in the following sections.

Walkie Stacker
A walkie stacker (see Figure 5-12) enables a pallet to be lifted, stacked, and transported short distances. The operator steers from a walking position behind the vehicle. In a situation where there is low throughput, short travel distances and low vertical storage height, and a low cost solution is desired, the walkie stacker may be appropriate. A typical walkie stacker can stack loads a maximum of three loads high, costs in the range of $10,000 and offers the dual purpose (no handoff required) of pallet retrieval/putaway and truck loading/unloading.

Counterbalanced Lift Trucks
As the name implies, counterbalance lift trucks (see Figure 5-13) employ a counterbalance in the back of the truck to stabilize loads carried and lifted on a mast in the front of the truck. Counterbalance lift trucks may be gas or battery powered. Besides forks, other attachments may be used to lift unique

FIGURE 5-12   A walkie stacker.
Source: Crown

FIGURE 5-13   A counterbalance lift truck.
Source: Hyster

load configurations on a vertical mast. The height limitation is generally around 25 feet. A counterbalanced truck may not be used to store double deep. Counterbalance trucks are available with operating capacities up to 100,000 pounds and cost in the range of $30,000.

Because the operator rides (seated or standing in the case of stand-up counterbalance trucks) on the vehicle, counterbalance trucks can be used for longer moves than walkie stackers. Counterbalance trucks also offer the flexibility to retrieve/putaway a pallet and load/unload a truck in the same move. This flexibility, coupled with the vehicle's relatively low cost, make the counterbalance lift truck the benchmark for all other pallet retrieval vehicles.

The major drawback of the counterbalance lift truck is the wide turning radius required to turn the vehicle in an aisle. As a result, an 11 to 12 feet storage aisle width is typically required. This aisle width requirement is the justification focus of alternative vehicles. As we proceed through the remaining list, the vehicles will offer progressively narrower storage aisles (hence, the reference to *narrow aisle vehicles*) and progressively taller reaching heights. At the same time, the vehicles are progressively more expensive and none offer the retrieval/putaway-load/unload flexiblity that the counterbalance truck offers. Thus, the incremental space savings and cost must be sufficient to pay for the incremental vehicle cost and loss of handling flexibility.

As selective pallet rack is the benchmark pallet storage mode, the counterbalanced truck may be considered the benchmark storage/retrieval vehicle. When it is desirable to use the same vehicle for loading/unloading trucks and storing/retrieving loads, the counterbalanced truck is the logical choice. For use in block stacking, drive-in and drive-thru rack and pallet stacking frames, the operating aisles normally provided are suitable for counterbalanced trucks.

Multiload counterbalance trucks (see Figure 5-14) can be used to increase the overall productivity of lift truck operations.

Straddle Trucks

A straddle truck (see Figure 5-15) provides load and vehicle stability using outriggers to straddle the pallet load, instead of counterbalanced weight. As a result, the aisle width requirement is 8 to 10 feet as opposed to 11 to 12 feet required with a counterbalance truck. To access loads in storage, the outriggers are driven into the rack, enabling the mast to come flush with the pallet face. Hence, it is necessary to support the floor level load on rack beams. A typical straddle truck costs in the range of $35,000.

FIGURE 5-14   A multiload counterbalance truck.

FIGURE 5-15   A straddle truck.

Straddle Reach Trucks

Straddle reach trucks (see Figure 5-16) were developed from conventional straddle trucks by shortening the outriggers on the straddle truck and providing a "reach" capability with a scissor reach mechanism. In so doing, the outriggers do not have to be driven under the floor level load to enable access to the storage positions. Hence, no rack beam is required at the floor level, conserving rack cost and vertical storage requirements.

Two basic straddle reach truck designs are available: mast and fork reach trucks. The mastreach design consists of a set of tracks along the outriggers that support the mast. The forkreach design consists of a pantograph or scissors mounted on the mast.

The double-deep reach truck, a variation of the forkreach design, enables the forks to be extended to a depth that permits loads to be stored two deep. A typical straddle reach truck operates in an 8 to 10 feet aisle and costs in the range of $40,000.

FIGURE 5-16   **A straddle reach truck.**
Source: Hyster

Sideloading Trucks

A sideloading truck (see Figure 5-17) loads and unloads from one side, thus eliminating the need to turn in the aisle to access storage positions. There are two basic sideloader designs. Either the entire mast moves on a set of tracks transversely across the vehicle, or the forks project from a fixed mast on a pantograph.

Aisle width requirements are less than for straddle trucks and reach trucks. A typical aisle would be 6 1/2 feet wide, rail or wire guided. Sideloaders can generally access loads up to 40 feet high and cost in the range of $65,000.

The major drawback of the sideloader truck is the need to enter the correct end of the aisle to access a particular location, thus adding to the time and complexity involved in truck routing. Turret trucks are designed to address this shortcoming while offering all of the other benefits of sideloader trucks.

FIGURE 5-17   A sideloader truck.
Source: Raymond

A variety of load types can be handled using a sideloader. The vehicle's configuration particularly lends itself to storing long loads in cantilever rack.

Turret Trucks

Turret trucks (swingmast and swingreach models) do not require the vehicle to make a turn within the aisle to store or retrieve a pallet (see Figure 5-18). Rather, the load is lifted either by forks that swing on the mast, a mast that swings from the vehicle, or a shuttle fork mechanism.

Turret trucks provide access to load positions at heights up to 50 feet, which provides the opportunity to increase storage density where floor space is limited. They can also run in aisles 5 or 6 feet wide, further increasing storage density.

FIGURE 5-18   **A turret truck.**
Source: Crown

Turret trucks generally have good maneuverability outside the aisle, and some of the designs with telescoping masts may be driven into a shipping trailer.

Because narrow aisle side reach trucks do not turn in the aisle, the vehicle may be wire guided or the aisles may be rail guided, enabling for greater speed and safety in the aisle and reducing the chances of damage to the vehicle and/or rack. A typical turret truck costs in the range of $80,000.

Hybrid Storage/Retrieval (S/R) Vehicles

A hybrid S/R vehicle (see Figure 5-19) is similar to a turret truck, except that the operator's cab is lifted with the load. The hybrid vehicle evolved from the design of an automated storage and retrieval machine used in automated storage/retrieval systems. Unlike the AS/RS machine, a hybrid truck is not captive to an aisle, but may leave one aisle and enter another. Present models available are somewhat clumsy outside the aisle, but operate within the aisle at a high throughput rate.

FIGURE 5-19   A hybrid truck.

Hybrid vehicles operate in aisle widths ranging from 5 to 7 feet, enable rack storage up to 60 feet high in a rack supported building, and may include an enclosed operator's cab that may be heated and/or air conditioned.

Sophisticated hybrid vehicles are able to travel horizontally and vertically simultaneously to a load position. The lack of flexibility, the high capital commitment, and high dimensional tolerance in the rack are the disadvantages of hybrid vehicles.

A typical hybrid storage/retrieval vehicle costs in the range of $100,000.

Automated Storage/Retrieval Systems

An automated storage/retrieval system (see Figure 5-20) for pallets is commonly referred to as a unit load AS/RS. It is defined by the AS/RS product section of the Material Handling Institute as a storage system that uses fixed-path storage and retrieval (S/R) machines running on one or more rails between fixed arrays of storage racks.

FIGURE 5-20   Automated storage and retrieval system.

A unit load AS/RS usually handles loads in excess of 1,000 pounds and is used for raw material, work-in-process, and finished goods. The number of systems installed in the United States is in the hundreds, and installations are commonplace in all major industries.

A typical AS/RS operation involves the S/R machine picking up a load at the front of the system, transporting the load to an empty location, depositing the load in the empty location, and returning empty to the *input/output* (I/O) point. Such an operation is called a *single command* (SC) operation. Single commands accomplish either a storage or a retrieval between successive visits to the I/O point. A more efficient operation is a *dual command* (DC) operation. A dual command involves the S/R machine picking up a load at the I/O point, traveling loaded to an empty location (typically the closest empty location to the I/O point), depositing the load, traveling empty to the location of the desired retrieval, picking up the load, traveling loaded to the I/O point, and depositing the load. The key idea is that in a dual command, two operations, a storage and a retrieval, are accomplished between successive visits to the I/O point.

A unique feature of the S/R machine travel is that vertical and horizontal travel occur simultaneously. Consequently, the time to travel to any destination in the rack is the maximum of the horizontal and vertical travel times required to reach the destination from the origin. Horizontal travel speeds are on the order of 700 feet per minute; vertical travel speeds are on the order of 200 feet per minute.

The typical unit load AS/RS configuration, if there is such a thing, would include unit loads stored one deep (that is, single deep), in long narrow aisles, each of which contains a S/R machine. The one I/O point would be located at the lowest level of storage and at one end of this system.

More often than not, however, one of the parameters defining the system is atypical. The possible variations include the depth of storage, the number of S/R machines assigned to an aisle, and the number and location of I/O points.

When the variety of loads stored in the system is relatively low, throughput requirements are moderate to high, and the number of loads to be stored is high, it is often beneficial to store loads more than one deep in the rack. Alternative configurations include

- **Double-deep storage with single-load width aisles** Loads of the same SKU are typically stored in the same location. A modified S/R machine is capable of reaching into the rack for the second load.

- **Double-deep storage with double-load-width aisles**   The S/R machine carries two loads at a time and inserts them simultaneously into the double-deep cubicle.
- **Deep lane storage with single-load-width aisles**   An S/R machine dedicated to storing will store material into the lanes on either side of the aisle. The lanes may hold up to ten loads each. On the output side, a dedicated retrieval machine will remove material from the racks. The racks may be dynamic, having gravity or powered conveyor lanes.
- *Rack entry module* **(REM)**   Systems in which a REM moves into the rack system and places/receives loads onto/from special rails in the rack.

Another variation of the typical configuration is the use of transfer cars to transport S/R machines between aisles. Transfer cars are used when the storage requirement is high relative to the throughput requirement. In such a case, the throughput requirement does not justify the purchase of an S/R machine for each aisle, yet the number of aisles of storage must be sufficient to accommodate the storage requirement.

A third system variation is the number and location of I/O points. Throughput requirements or facility design constraints may mandate multiple I/O points at locations other than the lower left-hand corner of the rack. Multiple I/O points might be used to separate inbound and outbound loads and/or to provide additional throughput capacity. Alternative I/O locations include the type of the system at the end of the rack (some AS/RS are built underground) and the middle of the rack.

A typical AS/RS machine costs in the range of $300,000.

Automated Storage/Retrieval Vehicles

Automated storage/retrieval vehicles (see Figure 5-21) are driverless counterbalance trucks. ASR vehicles receive communication through and run on a grid of wires buried a fraction of an inch beneath the surface of warehouse floor. ASR vehicles are rare but can be justified when wage rates are high, when labor is scarce, and when move rates are high, stable, and over predictable paths. ASR vehicles cost in excess of $100,000.

Pallet Retrieval Systems Comparison and Selection

Table 5-2 presents a summary comparison of the key features of pallet retrieval systems.

FIGURE 5-21   Automated storage/retrieval vehicle.

TABLE 5-2   Pallet Retrieval Systems Comparison

	Counter-balance	Straddle	Straddle Reach	Side-loader	Turret	Hybrid	ASRS
Vehicle cost	$30,000	$35,000	$40,000	$75,000	$95,000	$125,000	$200,000
Lift height capacity	22'	21'	30'	30'	40'	50'	75'
Aisle width	10–12'	7–9'	6–8'	5–7'	5–7'	5'	4.5'
Weight capacity	2–10k	2–6k	2–5k	2–10k	3–4k	2–4k	2–5k
Lift speed	80 fpm	60 fpm	50 fpm	50 fpm	75 fpm	60 fpm	200 fpm
Travel Speed	550 fpm	470 fpm	490 fpm	440 fpm	490 fpm	490 fpm	700 fpm

5.3   PALLET STORAGE/RETRIEVAL SYSTEMS SELECTION

Pallet storage and retrieval systems should be selected in conjunction with one another to provide high storage density and high storage/retrieval throughput capacity. Because each item has unique demand and dimensional profiles and because each storage/retrieval system provides different storage/handling capabilities, the key is to determine the proper storage/retrieval combination for each item. To assist our clients in making this determination, we developed the pallet slotting optimizer, which computes

FIGURE 5-22   Pallet storage/retrieval systems selection.
Source: LRI's Pallet Slotting Optimizer

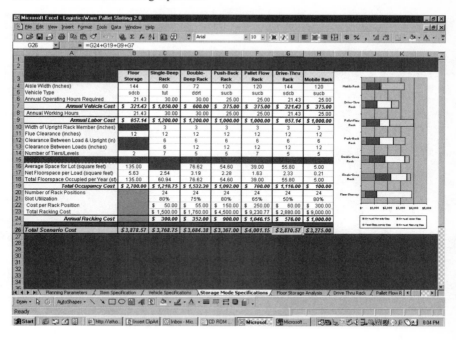

the lowest cost storage/retrieval alternative for each item in the warehouse, taking into consideration the cost of space, labor, racking, and equipment. An example analysis from a recent client engagement is provided in Figure 5-22.

6

CASE PICKING SYSTEMS

C ASE PICKING SYSTEMS CAN be organized into three categories. One category is pick face palletizing systems (see Section 6.1) where the order picker palletizes at the pick face as he or she traverses the picking tour. Another category is downstream palletizing systems (see Section 6.2) where cases are picked (manually or mechanically) onto conveyors, sorted into outbound orders, and palletized at or near the shipping dock. A third category is direct (or floor) loading systems (see Section 6.3) where cases are conveyed directly into outbound trailer loads without palletization. The pros, cons, applications, and related costs of each alternative are described here and are summarized in Table 6-1, which concludes the chapter.

6.1 PICK FACE PALLETIZING SYSTEMS

Pick face palletizing systems include pallet jack picking, pallet trains, lift truck picking, order picker trucks, end-of-aisle case picking, and robotic case picking.

Pallet Jack Picking

A pallet jack (see Figure 6-1) is a motorized vehicle equipped with forks to transport pallets at floor level. The operator rides on the front of the vehicle with the pallet secured by the forks on the back of the vehicle. A double pallet jack can carry two pallets at a time. Pallet jacks are by far the most popular method for case picking and are so common in the grocery industry that pallet jack picking is often referred to as the grocery picking method.

FIGURE 6-1 **Pallet jack picking.**
Source: Crown

The advantages of pallet jack picking are the low capital investment required, the simplicity of the concept, the flexibility, and safety since all of the picking takes place at floor level. Typical pallet jack picking rates range between 150 and 250 cases per person-hour. The cost of a typical pallet jack is around $8,000.

Double pallet jacks (see Figure 6-2) enable the operator to pick more than one pallet or more than one order at a time.

Pallet Trains
A train of pallets (see Figure 6-3) can be pulled behind a motorized vehicle to further increase the number of pallets or orders on a case picking tour.

Lift Truck Picking
Lift trucks (see Figure 6-4) are often overlooked as an option for case picking operations. Lift trucks are ideally suited to many case picking operations because the forks can be used to keep the top level of the pallet near the

C H A P T E R

FIGURE 6-2   Double pallet jack picking.
Source: Crown

FIGURE 6-3   Pallet trains.

FIGURE 6-4   **Lift truck picking.**

operator's waist level, to maneuver at high speed over long distances in the warehouse, and to load outbound trailers.

Order Picker Trucks

Order picker trucks (see Figure 6-5), sometimes referred to as stock pickers or cherry pickers, enable the order picker to travel to pick locations well above floor level. Because vertical travel velocity is much slower than horizontal travel velocity, and because the operator must take special care in positioning the vehicle in front of the pick location, the productivity of case picking with an order picker truck is only in the range of 50 to 100 cases per person-hour. (The productivity can be enhanced by minimizing vertical travel through popularity-based storage and/or intelligent pick tour construction.) Hence, order picker trucks are usually used for picking slow-moving items and where high-density storage is required. A typical order picker truck costs approximately $30,000.

End-of-Aisle AS/RS

Though rare, in some cases automated storage and retrieval systems (see Figure 6-6) are used to automatically convey pallet quantities to a stationary

FIGURE 6-5   Order picker truck.
Source: Crown

FIGURE 6-6   End-of-aisle case picking.

operator. The operator transfers the required number of cases from the storage pallet to the order pallet. Both pallets can be positioned such that the top of the pallet is at or near waist level for ease of handling. The advantages include high-storage density of the storage pallets, excellent ergonomics, and relatively high productivity because the operators are stationary. The disadvantages are the high degree of mechanization required and the associated capital investment and control complexities.

Robotic Case Picking

Recent developments in robot technology permit a robot to traverse a picking aisle, reach into a storage location, select a case or cases, and place the case or cases on a shipping pallet. Robotic case picking systems (see Figure 6-7) are rarely justifiable but may be in situations where labor is extremely scarce and/or expensive, when a relatively limited variety of carton sizes are picked, and in hazardous environments.

6.2   DOWNSTREAM PALLETIZING

Pick-to-belt, pick-car, automated case dispensing, and layer picking systems are used in downstream palletizing operations.

Pick-to-Conveyor

In the case of pick-to-conveyor (pick-to-belt) operations (see Figure 6-8), a conveyor runs the length of the case picking line, enabling the order picker

FIGURE 6-7   **Robotic case picking.**

FIGURE 6-8   **Case-pick-to-conveyor operation.**

to walk down the line removing cases from pallet storage locations and placing them on a take-away belt or roller conveyor. Typically, the operator applies a bar code label to each case as he removes it from its storage location. The bar code label is used for carton identification and downstream sortation of each case into its customer order.

The advantage of pick-to-conveyor operations (over pallet and order picker trucks) is a substantial increase in picking productivity, a result of pickers being confined to zones, less travel distance between picks, and the elimination of the order picker palletizing as they pick. The disadvantage is the need for a downstream sortation and palletizing system. Hence, there must be enough incremental productivity increase (pick-to-conveyor versus pallet jack picking) to pay for the additional handling steps and mechanization required.

Case Sorting Systems   In most pick-to-belt systems, cases must be sorted into outbound orders before they are palletized or loaded directly onto outbound trailers (see Figure 6-9). Pop-up wheels, pusher bars, shoes, or tilting trays can be used in conveyor systems to divert labeled cases into their appropriate accumulation lane.

FIGURE 6-9   Case sorting systems.

Pick-Car Systems

A pick-car (see Figure 6-10) is a telescoping conveyor belt attached to a man-aboard AS/RS machine operating within a picking aisle. The advantage over traditional pick-to-belt operations is the access to multiple picking levels and the ability to position the operator to pick and put at waist level.

Automated Case Dispensing

Automated case dispensing systems (see Figure 6-11) can be used to fully automate the putaway and retrieval of individual cases. In some systems, cases are housed in gravity flow racks. A shuttle table and a telescoping conveyor are attached to a vertical mast that travels on rails along the picking/putaway face. For putaway, a transport conveyor feeds individual cases to the telescoping conveyor. The cases travel up and along the telescoping conveyor to the putaway location. The shuttle table rides up the mast and horizontally with the mast to the putaway location. The telescoping conveyor feeds cases to the shuttle table, which in turn inserts cases in a gravity flow rack lane. The picking process is the putaway process in reverse.

FIGURE 6-10   **Pick-car system.**

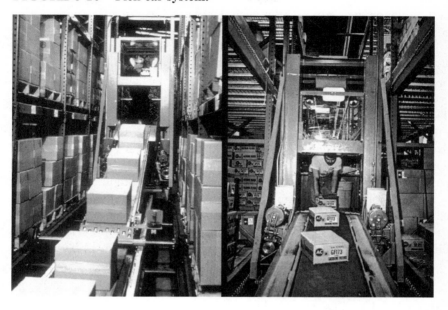

FIGURE 6-11   **Automated case dispensing system.**

The advantage of automated case dispensing is the complete elimination of human operators and the related labor and workman's compensation costs. The major drawback is the high maintenance requirements and the high initial investment. Each automated case dispensing mechanism costs approximately $500,000. An automated case dispensing mechanism can dispense approximately 500 cases per hour.

Tier (or Layer) Picking

Full-tier or layer picking systems (see Figure 6-12) are used to mechanically extract an entire layer of cases from a pallet. A variety of mechanical approaches for layer picking are available, including (1) vacuum suction and conveyor singulation of the top layer, (2) four-sided clamping and conveyor singulation, and (3) layer stripping conveyors, which literally lift up the front edge of the top layer and strip it away from the remaining layers.

The advantage of layer picking is the total elimination of human handling of the cases and high case-handling capacity. A typical layer picker

FIGURE 6-12   **Case layer picking.**

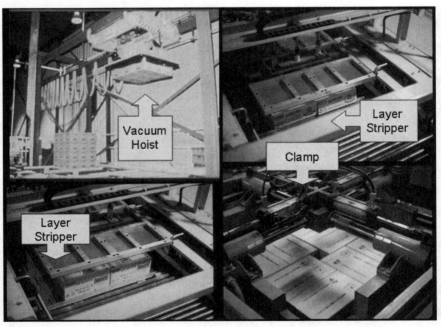

can handle between 750 and 1,000 cases per hour. The disadvantage is the high degree of mechanization and associated cost. As a result, layer pickers can typically only be justified when customers tend to order in high-volume, layer quantities and when the cost of labor is high.

Palletizing Systems
Once picked, cases can be palletized manually, mechanically, or robotically.

Manual Palletizing   Manual palletizing is often the only technically or financially feasible palletizing alternative (see Figure 6-13). Computerized pallet loading systems are now available to instruct palletizers in the optimal configuration of pallet loads with a wide variety of carton dimensions. The best systems generate pictograms of the optimal pallet configuration (see Figure 6-14). Lift and turn tables that keep the top of the shipping pallet at waist level significantly improve palletizing productivity and safety (see Figure 6-15).

Mechanical Palletizing   A conveyor-based mechanical palletizing system is illustrated in Figure 6-16. Mechanical palletizing systems are faster and safer than manual palletizing systems. They are much more expensive than manual palletizing systems and cannot work with the range of carton sizes that a manual palletizing system can.

FIGURE 6-13   Manual palletizing.

FIGURE 6-14   Optimal pallet load configuration.

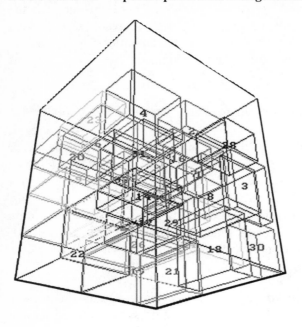

FIGURE 6-15   Lift and turn table.
Source: American Cancer Society

FIGURE 6-16   Mechanized palletizing.

Robotic Palletizing   Robotic palletizers (see Figure 6-17) can service a variety of shipping pallets at a time; however, they are not as fast as mechanical palletizers.

6.3   DIRECT LOADING SYSTEMS

When cases do not need to be palletized for shipping, they can be conveyorized directly into outbound trailers. A mechanized case loading system is illustrated in Figure 6-18. A robotic case loading system is illustrated in Figure 6-19.

6.4   CASE PICKING SYSTEMS SELECTION

A formal economic case picking mode analysis should be conducted to identify the appropriate combination of case picking systems. This analysis should consider the activity and inventory profile of each item and the storage and handling characteristics of each storage mode. The economic analysis should recommend the appropriate picking mode for each item based on

FIGURE 6-17   Robotic palletizer.

FIGURE 6-18   Conveyorized case loading.

FIGURE 6-19   Robotic case loading.

TABLE 6-1   Case Picking Systems Cost and Productivity Characteristics

	Picking Rates (Cases/Hour)	Initial Cost
Pallet Jack	100–250	$1k to $10k/vehicle
Order Picker Truck	50–100	$30k/vehicle
Pick to Roller	125–250	$1k/ft.
Pick to Belt	250–400	$200/ft + $2k/divert
End-of-Aisle AS/RS	200–300	$300k to $450k/aisle
Auto Extract	500–800	$200k/unit = $130/lane
Tier Picking	1,000–1,500	$150k/unit

this matching of item requirements and storage mode capabilities. We often used warehouse simulation tools to recommend the best designs. Table 6-1 presents the productivity and cost characteristics of each case-picking system alternative.

C H A P T E R

7

SMALL ITEM PICKING SYSTEMS

T
HE MAJOR TYPES OF BROKEN case picking systems are *picker-to-stock* (PTS) systems, *stock-to-picker* (STP) systems, and automated item picking. In picker-to-stock systems (see Section 7.1), the order picker walks or rides to the picking location. In stock-to-picker systems (see Section 7.2), the stock is mechanically (via carousel or AS/RS machine) transported to a stationary order picker. In automated item picking (see Section 7.3), items are automatically dispensed into shipping cartons or tote pans. In this chapter, we will describe the pros, cons, applications, and associated costs of each of these major system types. As before, we will move through the system descriptions in order of increasing cost, complexity, and degree of automation. This chapter concludes with a description of the techniques for choosing between the many equipment options for small item picking systems (see Section 7.4).

7.1 PICKER-TO-STOCK SYSTEMS

In picker-to-stock systems, the order picker walks or rides to the picking location. The two subsystems that must be selected are (1) the storage system that houses the stock and (2) the item retrieval system. The most popular alternatives for picker-to-stock storage systems and retrieval methods are reviewed in this section.

127

Picker-to-Stock Storage Systems

The three most popular picker-to-stock storage systems are bin shelving, modular storage drawers, and gravity flow rack.

Bin Shelving Systems   Bin (or metal) shelving systems (see Figure 7-1) are the oldest and still the most popular (in terms of sales volume dollars and the number of systems in use) equipment alternative for small parts order picking. Bin shelving systems are inexpensive ($100 to $150 per unit), easily reconfigured, and require very little if any maintenance.

Unfortunately, the lowest initial cost alternative may not be the most cost-effective alternative, or the alternative that meets the prioritized needs of a warehouse. With bin shelving systems, savings in initial cost and maintenance may be offset by inflated space and labor requirements.

Space is frequently underutilized in bin shelving systems, because the full inside dimensions of a shelving unit are rarely usable. Also, because people may be walking and extracting the items, the height of bin shelving units may be limited by the reaching height of a human being. As a result, the available building cube may also be underutilized.

The consequences of low space utilization are twofold. First, low space utilization means that a large amount of floorspace is required to store the products. The more expensive it is to own and operate the space, the more expensive low space utilization becomes. Second, the greater the floorspace,

FIGURE 7-1   Bin shelving.

the greater the area that must be traveled by the order pickers, and thus the greater the labor requirement and costs.

Two additional drawbacks of bin shelving are supervisory problems and item security/protection problems. Supervisory problems arise because it is difficult to supervise people through a maze of bin shelving units. Security and item protection problems arise because bin shelving is open; that is, all the items are exposed to and accessible from the picking aisles and by any operator and/or visitor.

Modular Storage Drawers/Cabinets   Modular storage drawers/cabinets (see Figure 7-2) are called modular because each storage cabinet houses modular storage drawers that are subdivided into modular storage compartments. Drawer heights range from 3 inches to 24 inches, and each drawer may hold up to 400 pounds worth of material. Storage cabinets can be thought of as shelving units that house storage drawers.

The primary advantage of storage drawers/cabinets over bin shelving is the large number of items that can be stored and presented to the order picker in a small area. A single drawer can hold from 1 to 100 items (depending on the size, shape, and inventory levels of the items), and a typical storage cabinet can store the equivalent of two to four shelving units worth of material. The excellent storage density accrues from the ability to create item

FIGURE 7-2   Modular storage drawers in cabinets.

housing configurations within a drawer/cabinet that very closely match the cubic storage requirements of each SKU. Also, because the drawers are pulled out into the aisle for picking, space does not have to be provided above each SKU to provide room for the order picker's hand and forearm. This reach space must be provided in bin shelving storage; otherwise, items deep in the unit cannot be accessed.

By housing more material in less floorspace, the overall space requirement for storage drawers is substantially less than that required for bin shelving. When the value of space is at a true premium, such as on a ship, on an airplane, on the manufacturing floor, or when facing the possibility of building additions, the reduction in space requirements alone can be enough to justify the use of storage drawers and cabinets.

Additional benefits achieved by the use of storage drawers include improved picking accuracy and protection for the items from the environment. Picking accuracy is improved over that in shelving units because the order picker's sight lines to the items are improved, and the quantity of light falling on the items to be extracted is increased. With bin shelving, the physical extraction of items may occur anywhere from floor level to seven feet off the ground, with the order picker having to reach into the shelving unit itself to achieve the pick. With storage drawers, the drawer is pulled out into the picking aisle for item extraction. The order picker looks down onto the contents of the drawer, which are illuminated by the light source for the picking aisle. (The fact that the order picker must look down on the drawer necessitates that storage cabinets be less than five feet in height.) Excellent item security and protection are achieved because the drawers can be closed and locked when not in use.

Storage cabinets equipped with drawers range in price from $1,000 to $1,500 per unit. Price is primarily a function of the number of drawers and the amount of sheet metal in the cabinet. Because the cost per cubic foot of storage is so high, storage drawers are only justifiable for items with very little on-hand cubic inventory (typically less than 0.5 cubic feet) and for operating scenarios in which the cost of space and the need for item security and protection are very high.

Gravity Flow Rack   Gravity flow rack (see Figure 7-3) is typically used for SKUs with high broken case cube movements and that are stored in fairly uniform sized and shaped cartons. Cartons are placed in the back of the rack from the replenishment aisle and advance/roll towards the pick face as cartons are depleted from the front. The back-to-front movement insures *first-in-first-out* (FIFO) turnover of the material.

FIGURE 7-3   Gravity flow rack picking operation.

Essentially, a section of flow rack is a bin shelving unit turned perpendicular to the picking aisle with rollers placed on the shelves. The deeper the sections, the greater the portion of warehouse space that will be devoted to storage, as opposed to aisle space. Further gains in space efficiency can be achieved by making use of the cubic space over the flow rack for full pallet storage.

Flow rack ranges in price from $3 to $10 per carton stored, depending on the length and weight capacity of the racks. As is the case with bin shelving, flow rack has very low maintenance requirements and is available in a wide variety of standard section and lane sizes from a number of suppliers.

The fact that just one carton of each line item is located on the pick face means that a large number of SKUs are presented to the picker in a small area. Hence, walking and therefore labor requirements can be reduced with an efficient layout. (To make sure that the space behind the front carton is properly utilized, only the SKUs with two or more cartons on-hand should be assigned to positions in gravity flow rack.)

Space Saving Systems   Mezzanines and mobile storage systems can be employed to improve the utilization of building cube and floorspace in picker-to-stock systems.

Mezzanines   Bin shelving, modular storage cabinets, flow rack, and even carousels can be placed on a mezzanine (see Figure 7-4). The advantage of

FIGURE 7-4   Mezzanine picking operation.

using a mezzanine is that nearly twice as much material can be stored in the original square footage. The major design issues for a mezzanine are the selection of the proper grade of mezzanine for the loading that will be experienced, the design of the material handling system to service the upper levels of the mezzanine, and the utilization of the available clear height. At least 14 feet of clear height should be available for a mezzanine to be considered. The cost of a typical mezzanine system is $10 to $20 per square foot.

The key to maintaining high-order picking productivity when a mezzanine is in use is to slot the products so that most of the picking activity takes place at the floor level. Consequently, the SKUs with the highest picking density should be assigned to the floor level and the SKUs with the lowest picking density should be assigned to the upper level. This ABC slotting policy with field picking of the upper level(s) should yield excellent picking productivity. (Field picking is wave picking the upper level(s) prior to picking from the floor level. The contents of the wave are housed in designated bins on the floor level. Those bins are one of the stops on the picking tours of the floor level.)

Mobile Storage Systems   Bin shelving, modular storage cabinets, and flow rack can all be "mobilized" (see Figure 7-5). The most popular method of mobilization is the "train-track" method. Parallel tracks are cut into the floor, and wheels are placed on the bottom of the storage equipment to create mobi-

FIGURE 7-5 Mobile storage system.

lized equipment. The space savings accrue from the fact that only one aisle is needed between all the rows of storage equipment. The aisle is created by separating two adjacent rows of equipment. As a result, the aisle "floats" in the configuration between adjacent rows of equipment.

The storage equipment is moved by simply sliding the equipment along the tracks, by turning a crank located at the end of each storage row, or by invoking electric motors that provide the motive power. The disadvantage to this approach is the increased time required to access the items. Every time an item must be accessed, the corresponding storage aisle must be created. Hence, mobile storage systems should only be used for very slow-moving items and when space is very scarce and/or expensive.

Picker-to-Stock Retrieval Methods

Picker-to-stock retrieval methods include cart picking, tote picking, man-aboard systems, and robotic item picking. The pros, cons, and applications of each are described in this section.

Cart Picking   A variety of picking carts (see Figures 7-6 through 7-8) is available to facilitate accumulating, sorting, and/or packing orders as an order picker makes a picking tour. Conventional carts provide dividers for order sortation, a place to hold paperwork and marking instruments, and a step ladder for picking at levels slightly above reaching height. Batch picking carts

FIGURE 7-6   Traditional order picking cart.

are designed to enable an order picker to pick multiple orders on a picking tour, thus dramatically improving productivity as opposed to strict single-order picking for small orders. More sophisticated carts automatically transport an order picker to a pick location, use light displays to direct the order picker to sort the contents of a pick into the correct order position, and permit mobile online communications via RF links and/or wireless local area network links. Cart picking rates range from 70 to 120 lines per person-hour.

Tote (or Carton) Picking   In tote picking systems (see Figure 7-9), conveyors are used to transport tote pans (or shipping cartons) through successive picking zones to enable order completion. The tote pans are used to establish order integrity, for merchandise accumulation and containment, and/or for shipping. Order pickers may walk one or more totes through a single picking zone, partially completing several orders at a time, or an order picker may walk one or more totes through all picking zones, thus completing one or more orders on each pass through the picking zones. Tote picking rates range from 150 to 300 lines per person-hour. The improvement over cart picking must be sufficient to justify the additional investment in conveying and sorting systems.

FIGURE 7-7 **Picking cart with on-board infrared communications, sort-by-light, and smart card readers.**

Man-up Systems   In the systems described thus far, the operator remains at floor level. To improve the utilization of building cube and floorspace, order pickers can ride up on an order picker truck or a man-aboard AS/RS machine to locations as high as 40 to 50 feet. The operation of order picker trucks was explained in Chapter 6, "Case Picking Systems." The operation of a man-aboard AS/RS is described in this section.

A man-aboard AS/RS (see Figure 7-10), as the name implies, is an automated storage and retrieval system in which the picker rides aboard a storage/retrieval machine to the pick locations. The storage locations may be provided by stacked bin shelving units, stacked storage cabinets, and/or a pallet rack. The *storage/retrieval* (S/R) machine may be aisle captive or free roaming.

Typically, the order picker leaves from the front of the system at floor level and visits enough storage locations to fill one or multiple orders, depending on the order size. The order picker can sort on board if enough containers are provided on the S/R machine.

FIGURE 7-8   Picking cart with on-board computing, sort-by-light, and on-board weigh counting.

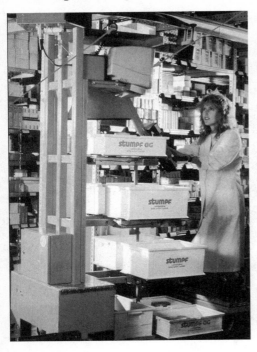

FIGURE 7-9   Tote picking system.

FIGURE 7-10   **Man-aboard AS/RS picking operation.**

A man-aboard AS/RS offers significant floorspace savings over the systems described so far. The floorspace savings are available because the storage system heights are no longer limited by the reach height of the order picker. Shelves or storage cabinets can be stacked as high as floor loading, weight capacity, throughput requirements, and/or ceiling heights will permit. The keys to achieving good picking productivity are intelligent slotting and pick tour sequencing. If there are ten or fewer picks per aisle traversal, then the objective is to keep most of the picks at or near floor level. If there are more than ten picks per aisle traversal, the operator should most likely be sequenced to make a sweep of the upper and lower levels of the aisle. In that case, bands of fast-moving items should be located in the upper and lower levels. The operator should traverse along the lower band on the way out from the I/O point and along the upper band on the way back to the I/O point.

Man-aboard automated storage and retrieval systems are far and away the most expensive picker-to-stock equipment alternative. Aisle-captive storage/retrieval machines reaching heights up to 40 feet cost around $125,000. Hence, there must be enough storage density and/or productivity improvement over cart and tote picking to justify the investment. Also, because vertical travel is slow compared to horizontal travel, typical picking rates in man-aboard operations range between 40 and 250 lines per person-hour. The range is large because there is a wide variety of operating schemes for man-aboard systems. Man-aboard systems are typically appropriate for slow-moving items where space is fairly expensive.

Robotic Item Picking   Robotic picking vehicles (see Figure 7-11) travel automatically through a sequence of picking locations receiving power and communication from rails in the floor and ceiling. The vehicles are equipped with a small carousel to permit order sortation, accumulation, and containment. The carousel travels up and down a mast on the robot as it traverses the picking aisle(s). The robot can automatically extract a storage drawer from a storage location onto the picking vehicle. The robot's arm is guided by an on-board vision system to direct item picking from a specific storage compartment in a storage drawer. Only in rare instances are robotic item picking systems justifiable.

FIGURE 7-11   Robotic item picking.

7.2   STOCK-TO-PICKER SYSTEMS

The two major types of stock-to-picker systems are carousels and miniload automated storage/retrieval systems. Each system type is described in this section.

The major advantage of stock-to-picker systems over picker-to-stock systems is the elimination of the travel time for the order picker. When wage rates are high, the labor savings can be sufficient to justify the investment in the mechanical and control systems required in stock-to-picker systems. If a stock-to-picker system is not designed properly, an order picker may remain idle waiting on the system to present the next picking transaction. In those cases, productivity can actually be worse than that found in picker-to-stock systems.

Another advantage of stock-to-picker systems is supervision. In stock-to-picker systems, the picking takes place at the end of an aisle. Hence, all of the operators should be visible to a supervisor in one quick glance down a picking line.

Carousels

Carousels, as the name implies, are mechanical devices that house and rotate items for order picking. Horizontal and vertical carousels are popular for order picking applications.

Horizontal Carousels   A horizontal carousel (see Figure 7-12) is a linked series of rotating bins of adjustable shelves driven on the top or on the bottom by a drive motor unit. Rotation is about an axis perpendicular to the floor at a rate of about 80 to 120 feet per minute.

Items are extracted from the carousel by order pickers who occupy fixed positions in front of the carousel(s). Order pickers may also be responsible for controlling the rotation of the carousel. Manual control is achieved via a keypad that tells the carousel which bin location to rotate forward and a foot pedal that releases the carousel to rotate. Carousels are normally computer-controlled, in which case the sequence of pick locations is stored in a computer and brought forward automatically.

The assignment of order pickers to carousels is flexible. If an order picker is assigned to one carousel unit, he or she must wait for the carousel to rotate to the correct location between picks. If an order picker is assigned to two or more carousels, he or she may pick from one carousel while the other is rotating to the next pick location. Remember, the objective of stock-to-picker systems is to keep the picker picking. (Humans are excellent extractors of items; the flexibility of our limbs and muscles provides us with this capability. We are not efficient searchers, walkers, or waiters.)

FIGURE 7-12   Horizontal carousel system.
Source: White

Horizontal carousels vary in length from 15 feet to 100 feet, and in height from 6 feet to 25 feet. The length and height of the units are dictated by the pick rate requirements and building restrictions. The longer the carousel, the more time required, on average, to rotate the carousel to the desired location. Also, the taller the carousel, the more time required to access the items. Heights over six feet require the use of ladders, lift platforms, or robot arms on vertical masts to access the items.

One drawback of horizontal carousels is that the throughput capacity is limited by the rotation speed of the motor drive. Another drawback is the initial investment of $40,000 to $70,000 per carousel unit. Consequently, items with a high cube movement should not be housed in carousels because the carousel may not be able to rotate fast enough to permit sufficient access to those items and because those items would occupy a large and expensive envelope of space in the carousel.

Vertical Carousels   A vertical carousel (see Figure 7-13) is a horizontal carousel turned on its end and enclosed in sheet metal. As with horizontal carousels, an order picker operates one or multiple carousels. The carousels are indexed either automatically via computer control or manually by the order picker working a keypad on the carousel's work surface.

FIGURE 7-13   Vertical carousel.
Source: Remstar

Vertical carousels range in height from 8 feet to 35 feet. Heights (as lengths were for horizontal carousels) are dictated by throughput requirements and building restrictions. The taller the system, the longer it will take, on average, to rotate the desired bin location to the pick station.

Order pick times for vertical carousels are theoretically less than those for horizontal carousels. The decrease results from the fact that items are always presented at an order picker's waist level. This eliminates the stooping and reaching with horizontal carousels, further reduces search time, and promotes more accurate picking. (Some of the gains in item extract time are negated by the slower rotation speed of the vertical carousel. Recall that the direction of rotation is against gravity.)

Additional benefits provided by the vertical carousel include excellent item protection and security. In the vertical carousel, only one shelf of items is exposed at one time, and the entire contents of the carousel can be secured.

The cost of a typical vertical carousel is around $100,000, increasing with the number of shelves, weight capacity, and special features and controls. The additional cost of vertical carousels over horizontal carousels is a result of the sheet metal enclosure, and the extra power required to rotate against the force of gravity.

Miniload Automated Storage and Retrieval Systems

In miniload automated storage and retrieval systems (see Figure 7-14), an automated storage/retrieval (S/R) machine travels horizontally and vertically simultaneously in a storage aisle, transporting storage containers to and from an order picking station located at one end of the system. The order picking station typically has two pick positions. As the order picker is picking from the container in the left pick position, the S/R machine is taking the container from the right pick position back to its location in the rack and returning with the next container. The result is that an order picker alternately picks from the left and right pick positions.

FIGURE 7-14   Miniload automated storage and retrieval system.

The sequence of containers to be processed can be determined manually (the order picker keys in the desired line item numbers or rack locations on a keypad) or automatically by computer control.

Miniloads vary in height from 8 to 50 feet, and in length from 40 to 200 feet. As in the case with carousels, the height and length of the system are dictated by the throughput requirements and building restrictions. The longer and taller the system, the longer the time required to access the containers. However, the longer and taller the system, the fewer the aisles and S/R machines that will have to be purchased. Since miniload systems lost between $150,000 and $300,000 per aisle, the determination of the correct system length, height, and number of aisles to meet the pick rate, storage, and economic return requirements for the warehouse is critical.

The transaction rate capacity of the miniload is governed by the capability of the S/R machine (which travels approximately 500 feet per minute horizontally and 120 feet per minute vertically) to continuously present the order picker with unprocessed storage containers. This capability, coupled with the human factor benefits of presenting the containers to the picker at waist height in a well-lit area, can yield pick rates ranging between 40 and 200 picks per person-hour.

Floorspace requirements are low due to the ability to store material up to 50 feet high, the ability to size and shape the storage containers and the subdivisions of those containers to very closely match the storage volume requirements of each SKU, and an aisle width that need only accommodate the width of a storage container.

As the most sophisticated of the system alternatives described thus far, it should come as no surprise that the miniload carries the highest price tag of any of the order picking system alternatives. Another result of its sophistication is the significant engineering and design time that accompanies each system. Most systems require between 6 and 12 months for design, delivery and installation. Finally, greater sophistication leads to greater maintenance requirements. It is only through a disciplined maintenance program that miniload suppliers are able to advertise up-time percentages between 97 and 99.5 percent.

Fortunately, a group of new miniload suppliers are making preengineered, modular systems. The new systems can be installed in a few months and are less expensive and more reliable than their predecessors.

7.3   AUTOMATED ITEM DISPENSING MACHINES

Automated item dispensing systems (see Figure 7-15) act much like vending machines for small items of uniform size and shape. Each item is allocated a vertical dispenser ranging from two to six inches wide and from three to five feet tall. (The width of each dispenser is easily adjusted to accommodate variable product sizes.) The dispensing mechanism acts to kick the unit of product at the bottom of the dispenser out onto a conveyor running between two rows of dispensers configured as an A-Frame over a belt conveyor. A tiny vacuum conveyor or small finger on a chain conveyor is used to dispense the items.

Virtual order windows begin at one end of the conveyor and pass by each dispenser. If an item is required in the order window, it is dispensed onto the conveyor. Merchandise is accumulated at the end of the belt conveyor into a tote pan or carton. A single dispenser can dispense at a rate of up to six units per second. Automatic item pickers are popular in industries with high throughput for small items of uniform size and shape, such as cosmetics, wholesale drugs, compact discs, videos, publications, and poly-bagged garments.

Replenishment is performed manually from the back of the system. The manual replenishment operation significantly cuts into the potential savings in picking labor requirements. Nonetheless, typical picking rates are in the range of 1,500 to 2,000 picks per person-hour. Typical picking accuracy is 99.97 percent.

FIGURE 7-15   **Automated item dispensing machine.**

7.4 BROKEN CASE PICKING SYSTEMS COMPARISON AND SELECTION

As is the case in all of the systems' selections and justifications described so far, a picking mode economic analysis should be conducted to assign each item to its most economically attractive storage mode. This analysis should consider the activity and inventory profile of each item and the storage and handling characteristics of each storage mode. The economic analysis should recommend the appropriate storage mode for each item based on matching each item's requirements to a storage mode's capabilities. The item slotting optimizer automates this selection process (see Figure 7-16). The tool calculates the picking, restocking, space, equipment, and error costs for each item in each potential storage mode. Table 7-1 presents the summary characteristics of each broken case picking system.

FIGURE 7-16   **Item slotting optimization.**
Source: LRI Slotting Optimizes

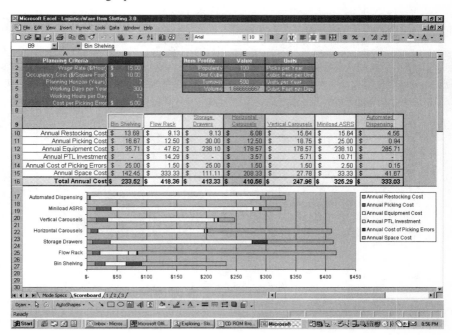

TABLE 7-1 Summary Characteristics of Alternative Broken Case Picking Systems

System Attribute	Unit of Measure	Bin Shelving	Gravity Flow Racks	Storage Drawers	Horizontal Carousel	Vertical Carousel	Miniload AS/RS	Automatic Dispersing
Gross system cost	Initial cost/purchased Ft3	$5–15	$3–5	$25–30	$20–35	$40–70	$30–40	$300–600 per dispenser
Net system cost	Initial cost/available Ft3	$10–30	$9–15	$31–38	$40–70	$65–100	$38–50	
Floorspace requirements	Ft3 of inventory housed per Ft2 of floorspace	1–1.2	0.7–0.85	1.8–2.5	0.8–1.25	5.0–6.0	4.0–5.0	
Human factors	Ease of retrieval	Average	Average	Good	Average	Excellent	Excellent	Good
Maintenance requirements		Low	Low	Low	Medium	Medium	High	High
Item security		Average	Average	Excellent	Good	Excellent	Excellent	Average
Flexibility	Ease to reconfigure	High	High	High	Medium	Low	Low	Low
Pick rate	Order lines per person-hour	C: 25–125, T: 100–350, M: 25–250, W: 300–500	C: 25–125, T: 100–350, M: 25–250, W: 300–500	C: 25–125, T: 100–350, M: 25–250, W: 300–500	50–250	50–300	25–125	500–1,000
Key		C = Cart picking	T = Tote picking	M = Man-aboard ASRS	W = Wave picking			

146

C H A P T E R

8

ORDER PICKING
OPERATIONS

RECENT SURVEY OF WAREHOUSING professionals identified order picking as the highest priority activity in the warehouse for productivity improvements. There are several reasons for their concern. First, order picking is the most costly activity in a typical warehouse (see Figure 8-1). A recent study in the United Kingdom revealed that 63 percent of all operating costs in a typical warehouse can be attributed to order picking. It should not be a surprise that order picking represents such a large portion of the warehouse operating costs. Order picking is the most labor-intensive function in the warehouse. It is not unusual to find a majority of the warehouse workforce in order picking. To combat the labor intensity, most of the material and information-handling systems in warehousing are devoted to the order picking function. In addition, many of the decision support systems and engineering projects in a warehouse are associated with order picking. Finally, many of the errors made in warehousing are made in the order picking function. Hence, order picking is often the major source of the cost of warehousing errors.

Second, the order picking activity has become increasingly difficult to manage. The difficulty arises from the introduction of new operating programs such as *just-in-time* (JIT), cycle time reduction, quick response, and new marketing strategies such as *micromarketing* and *megabrand* strategies. These programs require that (1) smaller orders be delivered to warehouse

147

FIGURE 8-1   Operating cost distribution in a typical warehouse.

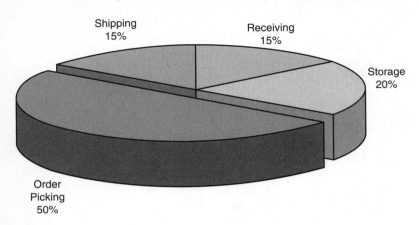

customers more frequently and more accurately, and that (2) more *stock keeping units* (SKUs) must be incorporated in the order picking system.

As a result, both throughput, storage, and accuracy requirements have increased dramatically. Third, renewed emphasis on quality improvements and customer service have forced warehouse managers to reexamine the order picking activity from the standpoint of minimizing product damage, reducing transaction times, and further improving picking accuracy. Finally, the conventional responses to these increased requirements to hire more people or to invest in more automated equipment have been stymied by labor shortages and high hurdle rates due to uncertain business environments. Fortunately, a variety of ways exist for improving order picking productivity without increasing staffing or making significant investments in highly automated equipment. The most effective of those improvement strategies are described and illustrated here:

- Issue pack optimization
- Pick-from-storage
- Pick task simplification
- Order batching
- Slotting optimization
- Pick sequencing

8.1   ISSUE PACK OPTIMIZATION

By encouraging customers to order in full-pallet quantities, or by creating quarter- and/or half-pallet loads, much of the counting and manual physical handling of cases can be avoided both in your warehouse and also in your customer's warehouse. In similar fashion, by encouraging customers to order in full-case quantities, much of the counting and extra packaging associated with loose case picking can be avoided. A pick line profile illustrating the distribution of the portion of a full pallet or full case requested by customers frequently reveals an opportunity to reduce the amount of partial pallet and/or partial case picking in the warehouse. An example profile was illustrated in Figure 2-4.

We recently helped a large retailer to determine their optimal carton quantities. Since stores were required to order in full-carton quantities, the larger the cartons, the fewer the picks in the warehouse. However, the larger the carton quantities, the greater the on-hand inventory levels in the stores. The tradeoff analysis incorporating warehouse picking costs and inventory carrying costs is illustrated in Figure 8-2.

8.2   PICK FROM STORAGE

A traditional U-shape warehouse layout (see Figure 8-3) incorporates receiving docks, receiving staging, receiving inspection, putaway to reserve storage,

FIGURE 8-2   Issue pack optimization.

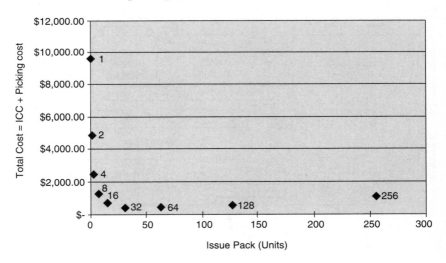

reserve pallet storage and pallet picking, case pick line replenishment from pallet storage, case picking, broken case pick line replenishment from case storage, broken case picking, packing, accumulation, shipping staging, and shipping docks.

Why do we need so many different storage and picking areas? Why do we need separate forward areas for case and broken case picking? The reason is that broken and full-case picking productivity from a large reserve pallet storage area is unacceptably low. The forward areas are small and compact, are uniquely configured for the picking task, and may have specialized equipment. As a result, the picking productivity in these areas is 10 to 20 times what the productivity would be in a large reserve storage area where the entire inventory for a single item would be housed. The picking productivity gain is almost always so great (as compared to picking from reserve storage locations) that the cost penalties paid for replenishing the forward areas, and the space penalty paid for establishing these stand alone areas are rarely considered.

FIGURE 8-3   Traditional U-shape warehouse configuration.

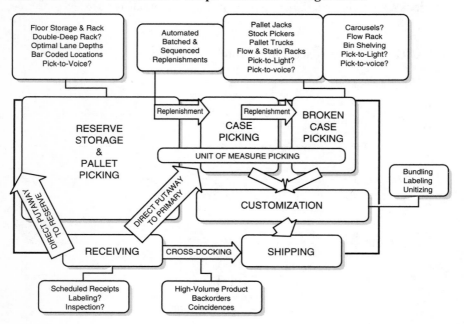

Now, suppose we could achieve forward picking rates from a reserve storage area? In so doing, we can have our cake and eat it too: excellent picking productivity, no forward area replenishment, and no extra space set aside for forward areas. Is it possible? It is in Ford's service parts distribution centers.

Ford Service Parts

At Ford's service parts distribution centers (see Figure 8-4), receipts arrive by rail in wire baskets, each identified with a bar code license plate. The wire baskets are moved by a lift truck operator to an automated receiving station. At the receiving station, the receiving operator scans the bar code to let the warehouse management system know that the item and cage are on site. The system then directs the operator to distribute the contents of the cage into one or more tote pans, each with a bar code license plate. Each tote is in turn assigned to and conveyed to one of 54 horizontal carousels for putaway by the carousel operator. The carousel operators each work a pod of three carousels. A real-time warehouse management system interleaves the putaway

FIGURE 8-4 Pick-from-storage order picking concept.

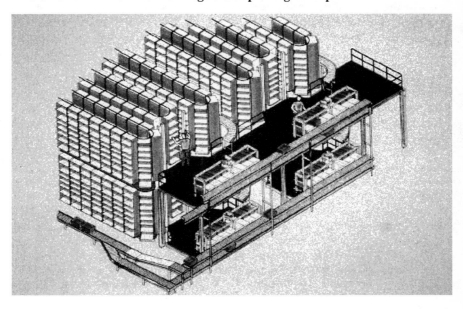

and picking tasks. All picking is light-directed and the operator is also light-directed to distribute each pick into order totes housed in flow rack adjacent to the carousels. Eighty percent of all part numbers and a corresponding portion of the activity in the DC is handled this way.

Is this picking from storage? Yes, because the 54 carousels act as the reserve storage area. The entire inventory for an item is housed in the carousel system, but not necessarily in the same carousel location. There is no replenishment within the system and there is no space set aside for back-up stock.

This operating concept gives Ford a significant competitive advantage in service parts logistics. The concept requires a highly sophisticated logistics information system (random storage, intelligent slotting, activity balancing, dynamic wave planning), a high degree of mechanization (to move the reserve storage locations to the order picker), and a disciplined workforce. This operating philosophy is not meant for every situation, but when the operating volumes are large enough, and the necessary resources are available, the pick-from-storage concept can yield tremendous productivity gains.

Because a majority of a typical order picker's time is spent travelling and/or searching for pick locations, one of the most effective means for improving picking productivity and accuracy is to bring the storage locations to the picker, preferably reserve storage locations. A large cosmetics distributor recently installed systems that bring reserve storage locations to stationary order picking stations for batch picking of partial-case quantities and direct induction into a cross-belt sortation system (see Figure 8-5). In so doing, order picking travel time has been virtually eliminated. In addition, the same system can transfer storage locations to or from receiving, prepackaging, and inspection operations, virtually eliminating travel throughout the warehouse. Though expensive, the systems may be justified by increased productivity and accuracy.

8.3 PICK TASK SIMPLIFICATION

Eliminate and combine order picking tasks when possible.

The human work elements involved in order picking may include the following:

- *Traveling* to, from, and between pick locations
- *Extracting* items from storage locations
- *Reaching* and *bending* to access pick locations

FIGURE 8-5   Pick-from-storage concept for health and beauty aids.

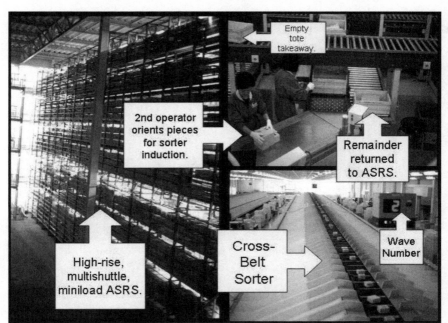

- *Documenting* picking transactions
- *Sorting* items into orders
- *Packing* items
- *Searching* for pick locations

A typical distribution of the order picker's time among these activities is provided in Figure 8-6. The means for eliminating the work elements are outlined in Table 8-1.

When work elements cannot be eliminated, they can often be combined to improve order picking productivity. Some effective combinations of work elements are outlined in the following section.

Travelling and Extracting Items

Stock-to-picker (STP) systems such as carousels and the miniload automated storage/retrieval system are designed to keep order pickers extracting while a mechanical device travels to, from, and between storage locations, bringing pick locations to the order picker. As a result, a man-machine balancing

FIGURE 8-6   Typical distribution of an order picker's working time.

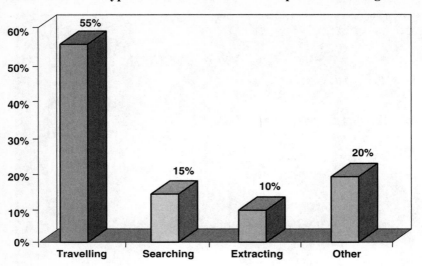

problem is introduced. If the initial design of stock-to-picker systems is not accurate, a significant portion of the order picker's time may be spent waiting on the storage/retrieval machine to bring pick locations forward.

Travelling and Documenting

Since a person-aboard storage/retrieval machine is programmed to automatically transport the order picker between successive picking locations, the order picker is free to document picking transactions, sort material, or pack material while the S/R machine is moving.

Picking and Sorting

If an order picker completes more than one order during a picking tour, picking carts equipped with dividers or totes may be designed to enable the picker to sort material into several orders at a time.

Picking, Sorting, and Packing

When the cube occupied by a completed order is small, say less than a shoe box, the order picker can sort directly into a packing or shipping container (see Figure 8-7). Packing or shipping containers must be set up ahead of time and placed on picking carts equipped with dividers and/or totes.

TABLE 8-1   Order Picking Work Elements and Means for Elimination

Work Element	Method of Elimination	Required Technology/ Functionality
Traveling	Bring pick locations to picker.	Stock-to-picker system: Miniload AS/RS Horizontal carousel Vertical carousel
Documenting	Automate information flow.	Computer-aided order picking Automatic identification systems Light-aided order picking Radio frequency terminals Headsets
Reaching	Present items at waist level.	Vertical carousels Person-aboard AS/RS Miniload AS/RS
Searching	Bring pick locations to picker. Take picker to pick location. Illuminate pick locations.	Stock-to-picker systems Person-aboard AS/RS Pick-to-light systems
Extracting	Automated dispensing.	Automatic item pickers Robotic order pickers
Counting	Weigh counting. Prepackage in issue increments.	Scales on picking vehicles
Restocking	Automated look ahead replenishment should insure that each location has a sufficient pick quantity before the order picker reaches the location.	Location min-max triggers
Excessive socializing	Assign operators to dedicated zones for picking and putaway.	
Idling/waiting for work	Dynamic zone sizing. Perpetual to-do lists.	Real-time WMS.

FIGURE 8-7   Pick and pack.

8.4   ORDER BATCHING

Batch orders to reduce total travel time.

By increasing the number of orders (and therefore items) picked by an order picker during a picking tour, the travel time per pick can be reduced. For example, if an order picker picks one order with two items while travelling 100 feet, the distance travelled per pick is 50 feet. If the picker picked two orders with four items, the distance travelled per pick is reduced to 25 feet.

Single line orders are a natural group of orders to pick together. Single line orders can be batched by small zones in the warehouse to further reduce travel time. A profile of the number of lines requested per order helps identify the opportunity for batching single line orders. An example profile is illustrated in Figure 8-8.

Other order batching strategies are depicted in the order batching decision tree and are described later in this section (see Figure 8-9). Note that when an order is assigned to more than one picker, the effort to reestablish

FIGURE 8-8   **Lines and cube per order profile used in batch-wave planning.**

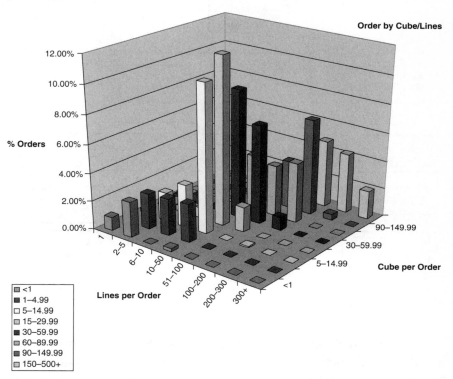

order integrity is significantly increased. The additional cost of sortation must be evaluated with respect to the travel time savings generated with batch picking.

Single Order Picking

In single order picking, each order picker completes one order at a time. For picker-to-stock systems, single order picking is like going through the grocery store and accumulating the items on your grocery list into your cart. Each shopper is concerned with only his or her list.

The major advantage of single order picking is that order integrity is never jeopardized. The major disadvantage is that the order picker is likely to have to travel over a large portion of the warehouse to pick a single order. Consequently, the travel time per line item picked is high if the order does

FIGURE 8-9   Order batching decision tree.

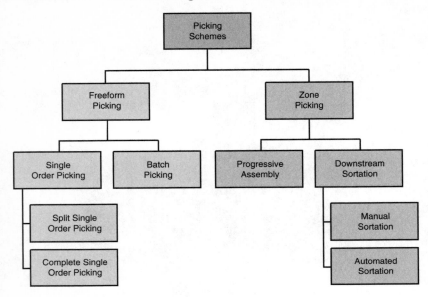

not contain several line items. For large orders (those greater than ten-line items), a single order may yield an efficient picking tour. In addition, in some systems, response time requirements do not allow orders to build up in a queue to create efficient batches for order picking. For an emergency order, the customer service motivation should override the efficiency motivation, and we should pick the single emergency order.

Batch Picking

A second operating strategy for order picking is batch picking. Instead of an order picker working on only one order at a time, orders are batched together. Order pickers take responsibility for retrieving a batch of orders during a picking tour. In the grocery store example, batch picking can be thought of as going to the grocery store with your shopping list and those of some of your neighbors. In one traversal of the grocery store, you will have completed several orders. As a result, the travel time per line item picked will be reduced by approximately the number of orders per batch. The major advantage of batch picking is a reduction in travel time per line item.

The major disadvantages of batch picking are the time required to sort line items into customer orders and the potential for picking errors.

Orders may be sorted in one of two ways. First, the order picker may use separate containers to sort the line items of different orders as he or she traverses the warehouse. Special pick carts and containers are available to facilitate this approach. Second, the line items and quantities of different orders may be grouped together to be sorted later. It is the cost of this sortation process, not required in strict order picking, that determines whether batch picking is a cost-effective strategy.

Batch picking can also be used in stock-to-picker systems. In those cases, all the line items requested in the batch of orders are picked from a location as it is presented to the picker. Again, the benefits of reduced travel time must be weighed against the cost of sortation and the potential for filling orders. Batch picking is especially effective for small orders (one- to five-line items).

Zone Picking

The first decision in order picking system design is whether or not to organize order picking by assigning operators to picking zones. A picking zone is defined as a portion of an aisle, multiple aisles, or machines (carousels or AS/RS machines) assigned to an operator for picking. The key distinguishing feature is that the operator is dedicated to a zone and no other operator works in that zone. In order picking, this also means that the operators do not have order completion accountability because the lines on an order will be filled from different zones and hence by different order pickers.

A storage zone is distinguished from a picking zone. Storage zones are defined to facilitate efficient and safe storage. For example, storage zones may be established for bulky items, floor storage items, small items, bar stock items, refrigerated items, frozen items, flammable items, explosive items, and so on. These zones are specified in slotting.

The opposite of zoning for order picking is free-form picking. In free-form picking, order pickers are responsible for picking every line on each order assigned to them and they are free to move to any aisle in the warehouse. The pros and cons of creating picking zones are highlighted in Table 8-2.

Xerox Service Parts

I recently toured a Xerox service parts distribution center outside of Chicago, Illinois. During the tour, I spent nearly an hour observing the order picking operation. In that operation, order pickers are each assigned to a zone of two

TABLE 8-2   To Zone or Not to Zone?

Zoning Pros	Notes and Comments
Operator travel time is reduced because operators are assigned to small dedicated work areas.	I always prefer to play zone defense in basketball because I do not have to chase anyone around the court and because I do not have responsibility for an opposing player's scoring outbursts.
Operators become familiar with the products and locations in their zone.	Product familiarity should yield improved picking productivity and picking accuracy. (See "Xerox Service Parts.")
Congestion is minimized because not more than one operator is in an aisle at a time.	Minimizing congestion is the most important justification for zone picking. In some operations, the volume is so great that free-form picking creates gridlock-like bottlenecks.
There is operator-zone accountability.	The order picking performance (productivity, accuracy, and housekeeping) can be recorded and posted by zone. The tradeoff is the loss in accountability for orders. (See "Cotter and Company, True Value Hardware.")
Minimizes excessive socializing.	Because operators are assigned alone to dedicated work zones, there is little or no opportunity during a pick wave for excessive socializing. Some socializing is healthy, but zone picking helps to control and monitor it.

long aisles of bin shelving. Orders are progressively assembled by conveying an order tote from zone to zone.

I especially enjoyed meeting the top performing order picker. She had been with Xerox for over 20 years and had worked the same two aisles in the warehouse for over 3 years. The housekeeping, productivity, and accuracy in her zone were the highest in the warehouse. Her pride in her job was also evident by the near-perfect arrangement of the merchandise in her zone.

I could not help but comment to her about the excellent performance record she had and on the neatness of her work area.

During the conversation, I noticed that the merchandise in the bin closest to the front of her zone and next to the takeaway conveyor was not nearly as neatly arranged as the other bins. It was so unusual compared to other bins in her zone that I asked her about the arrangement of that particular bin. She told me the bin contained merchandise that customers were going to order that day. How did she know that? She did not have ESP or claim to function as the world's greatest forecasting system. The items in that bin were A-movers that had not been properly reslotted. The order picker grew tired of traveling to the end of her zone for those popular items. She simply moved some of the inventory for those items close to the front of the zone. This simple process improvement would have been impossible without the product and location familiarity that comes with zone picking.

Cotter and Company, True Value Hardware

Cotter and Company is the logistics subsidiary of True Value Hardware. Each of its small-item order picking areas is configured in single aisle zones. A takeaway belt conveyor runs down the center of each zone, enabling an operator to make one pass through the zone during a pick wave. During a pass, each operator works with a roll of picking labels. The labels present items in location sequence to the order picker who picks an item, places a bar code label on the item, places the labeled item on the belt conveyor, and moves to the next location. The takeaway belt conveyor feeds a downstream sortation system that sorts the items coming from each zone into retail store orders. At the end of each zone, the performance statistics, including picking productivity, picking accuracy (via internal audit), and housekeeping for the zone, are posted. Talk about public accountability!

The benefits of zone picking—reduced travel time, minimal congestion, product-location familiarity, and operator-zone accountability—may or may not pay for the associated costs and inherent control complexities presented by zone picking. Table 8-3 describes some of those costs and control difficulties.

In deciding whether or not zone picking makes sense, I recommend a formal economic and feasibility evaluation of the two picking policies: zone versus free-form picking. The analysis should compare the best free-form picking design with a zone picking scheme. Zone picking will be the right answer if enough incremental benefits (productivity and congestion) will pay for the additional investment cost of the zone picking system. I encourage

TABLE 8-3   Zone Picking Costs and Control Complexities.

Zone Picking Costs and Control Challenges	Notes and Comments
Order assembly.	The major difficulty and cost factor in zone picking is the need to assemble the order across order picking zones. The two methods for order assembly, progressive assembly by passing the contents of the order from zone to zone and wave picking with downstream sortation, can be excessively expensive. They can also reduce the operating flexibility of the warehouse and significantly increase the level of sophistication of warehouse control systems.
Workload imbalances can create bottlenecks, gridlock, and low worker morale.	It is nearly impossible to perfectly balance the workload between zones on a daily basis. To do so requires advanced slotting techniques or as is the case with highly sophisticated zone picking schemes, dynamic floating zones are used. In those operations, the size of the zone varies as a function of the associated workload. In either case, the controls are an order of magnitude more complex than those used in free-form picking.

you to try to devise free-form picking schemes that are so productive that it becomes nearly impossible to justify the additional investments in material- and information-handling systems required by zone picking. If the zone picking scheme is justifiable when compared to a highly efficient free-form scheme, then you can be confident that the justification is correct. Another approach is to try to configure a zone picking scheme that does not require a major investment in material- and information-handling systems. An example of this approach is in place at Lanier Worldwide.

Lanier Worldwide

Lanier Worldwide is a multibillion dollar distributor of copiers, fax machines, and dictation equipment. A major portion of its revenue comes from service parts and supplies that support its installation base. For parts and supplies picking, Lanier has devised a manual wave-zone picking concept. Parts and supplies are stored in traditional bin shelving. Operators are assigned to zones of four aisles of shelving (see Figure 8-10). Orders are released to the picking floor in 20-minute waves, just long enough to allow efficient picking tours and just short enough to maintain the attention and sense of urgency of the order pickers.

Each order picker takes a specially designed picking cart through his/her zone. Each picking cart is subdivided into eight compartments. Before each picking tour, an empty tote labeled with that zone and operator's identification is placed in each of the eight containers. At the beginning of each wave, an order picker is given a pick list that walks the operator through his/her zone in location sequence. On each line on the pick list is the location, the item identification, the quantity to pick, and the number of the compartment (1 through 8) on the cart to place the item into.

At the end of a tour, each order picker brings his/her cart to a large storage rack that is subdivided into (you guessed it) eight compartments. Each operator puts his/her #1 tote in the #1 compartment, his/her #2 tote in the

FIGURE 8-10   Lanier manual wave picking concept.

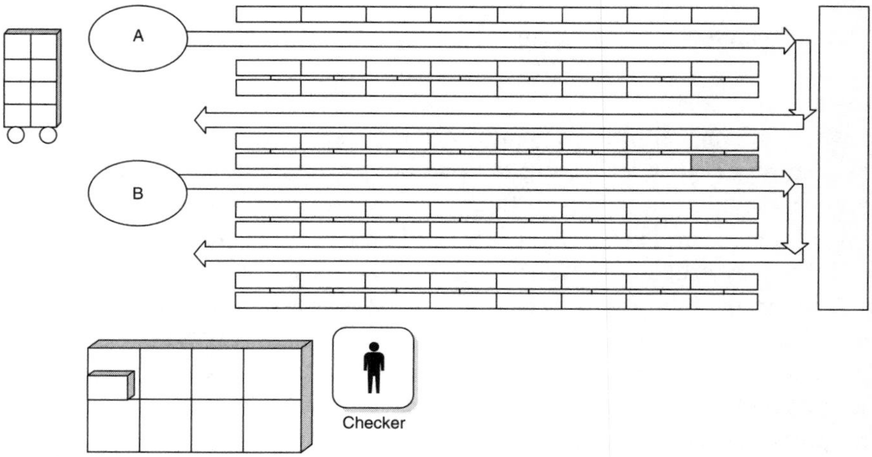

#2 compartment, and so on. Standing on the other side of the storage compartment is an operator whose job is to sort the merchandise in each compartment into orders, check the order for accuracy, and pack the contents of the order for shipping. This operation yields manual picking productivity in excess of 120 lines per person-hour and exceptionally high picking accuracy.

One advantage of zone picking is travel time savings. Because each picker's coverage has been reduced from the entire warehouse to a smaller area, the travel time per line item should be reduced from that of strict order picking. Again, however, these travel time reductions must be weighed against the costs of sorting and the potential for order-filling errors. Additional benefits of zone picking include the order picker's familiarity with the product in his or her zone, reduced interference with other order pickers, and increased accountability for productivity and housekeeping within the zone.

Two methods for establishing order integrity in zone picking systems are progressive assembly and downstream sortation.

Progressive Order Assembly

In progressive assembly (or pick-and-pass) systems, the contents of an order are passed from one zone to the next until the order is completely assembled (see Figure 8-11). The contents of the order may move in a tote pan or carton on a conveyor from zone to zone, they may be manually moved on a cart from zone to zone, or they may move on pallets on a towline conveyor, automated guided vehicle, lift truck, or pallet jack from zone to zone. Intelligent progressive order assembly systems will only move an order's container to a zone if there is a SKU for the order in that particular zone. This practice is called *zone skipping*.

Downstream Sortation

In wave picking with downstream sortation (see Figure 8-12), there is no designation of an order during the picking process. Order pickers work in parallel, making full passes of their pick zone during a wave. A product is typically bar code-labeled as it is picked and is placed into a large cart or onto a conveyor belt that passes alongside the pick line. The contents of the cart and/or the items on the takeaway conveyor are then inducted into a sortation system that sorts the merchandise into customer orders. The cost of downstream sortation systems can run into the millions of dollars. Hence, the incremental benefits of wave picking with downstream sortation compared to progressive order assembly must be sufficient to justify the incremental investment. The incremental benefits are primarily picking

FIGURE 8-11   Progressive order assembly with carousels.
Source: White

PICK & PASS CONCEPT

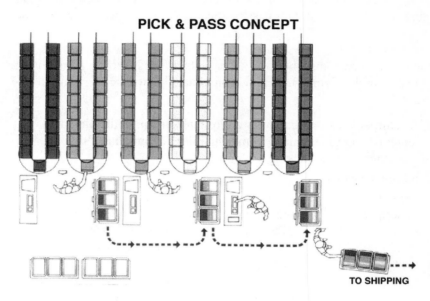

TO SHIPPING

FIGURE 8-12   Downstream sortation—picking from carousels.
Source: White

PARALLEL PICKING CONCEPT

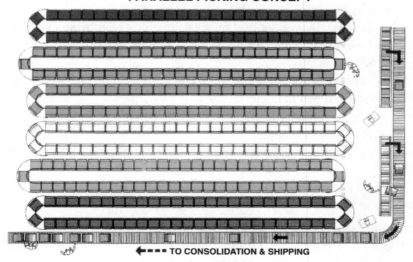

◀---- TO CONSOLIDATION & SHIPPING

productivity benefits. The incremental cost is the difference between the cost of the material- and information-handling systems required for downstream sorting versus that required for passing the order contents from zone to zone.

8.5 MUTOH

Mutoh's mail order distribution center outside of Nagoya, Japan, is an excellent example of zone picking with automated downstream sortation (see Figure 8-13).

1.   A returnable carton is used as a physical kanban, indicating a replenishment is required from a supplier, the inbound shipping container, and the picking carton.

2.   Inbound cartons flow directly from inbound trailers into a miniload AS/RS.

3.   Picking aisles are on mezzanines on the opposite side of the storage/retrieval aisle. Picking occurs on two shifts. During the third shift, the AS/RS machine reconfigures the entire pick line for the next day's picking activity.

4.   Each piece has a bar code label and pickers apply a bar code label to each polybagged garment as it is picked into a picking cart.

5.   A simple batch picking cart holds two corrugated totes.

6.   Order pickers work in dedicated picking zones; one aisle is one zone.

7.   Once full, each completed corrugated tote is conveyed to a sorter induction station. The contents of each tote are spilled into an induction station.

8.   Induction operators orient each piece so that it is read by an overhead bar code scanner by which each piece is assigned to a section on a cross-belt sorter.

9.   The cross-belt sorter conveys each piece to its assigned packing lane and diverts it down the lane.

10.   Packers move among the three or four lanes assigned to them and sort several pieces into their orders, pack them, and place them on an outbound shipping conveyor running below the bottom of the sorting lane.

11.   A mobile packing station makes it easy to move easily between sortation lanes.

To decide from among the four picking policies, I recommend that a concept be developed, evaluated, and sometimes simulated for each of the four picking paradigms. Beginning with single order picking and moving to batch

FIGURE 8-13   **Zone picking with automated downstream sortation.**

picking, then to progressive order assembly, and then to wave picking with downstream sortation, an incremental justification of the concepts should be conducted. From that justification process, a policy should be selected and implemented. Whatever the justified policy, the flexibility to single order pick and batch pick based on the characteristics of certain orders should be designed into the system.

8.6 SLOTTING OPTIMIZATION

In *slotting,* we determine for each item its

- Appropriate storage mode
- Appropriate allocation of space in its appropriate storage mode
- Appropriate storage location in its appropriate storage mode

As a result, slotting has a significant impact on all of the *warehouse key performance indicators* (WKPIs): productivity, shipping accuracy, inventory accuracy, dock-to-stock time, warehouse order cycle time, storage density, and the level of automation. Hence, few decisions do more to determine the overall performance of a warehouse than slotting. Nonetheless, very few warehouse management systems and very few warehouses have the data, let alone the engineering and computer support to intelligently slot the warehouse and to keep the slotting aligned with the current warehouse activity profile. (Some recent research suggests that less than 15 percent of the items in a typical warehouse are slotted correctly.) Consequently, most warehouses are spending 10 to 30 percent more per year than they should because the warehouse is improperly slotted.

Most warehouses are improperly slotted for many reasons: the data is not available, the MIS resources are not available, there is no way to keep the slotting current, there is no methodology for slotting, and so on. Here we will try to eliminate these excuses by presenting a methodology that is implemented on a personal computer attached to a host or stand-alone warehouse management system that recommends the appropriate slotting for a warehouse on an ongoing basis. The ten-step methodology is outlined in the following sections.

This intelligent slotting methodology is based on many years of research in slotting and recent slotting projects with Adolph Coors, Allied Signal, Arrow Electronics, Baptist Sunday School Board, Cardone Industries, Coats & Clark, DuPont, Mack Trucks, Nashua, Northern Telecom, PepsiCo, Polygram, Spartan Stores, and Stihl Corporation. After looking back on all those projects and all those different types of items (cans, bottles, and kegs of beer;

rolls of carpet backing; brake parts; spools of yarn; computer hardware and software; vials of nuclear medicine; automotive service parts; paper products; telecommunications equipment and parts; frozen food; cassettes and compact discs; perishable food items; and chainsaws), I identified the common denominators of the projects and developed this ten-step slotting methodology and supporting PC tool to assist in slotting projects in nearly any industry. An outline of the slotting methodology and example output from the Item Slotting Optimizer follows.

1. Conduct a Warehouse Operations Audit

The warehouse operations audit includes a warehouse performance and warehouse practices gap analysis (refer to Chapter 3, "Measuring and Benchmarking Warehouse Performance"). The purpose of the audit is to reveal if and how slotting could improve the operations of the warehouse. In some warehouse operations, intelligent slotting will not improve the performance of the operation because of poor management, poor worker morale, an undisciplined workforce, union-management tensions, poor housekeeping, inadequate computer training and support, and/or a variety of other reasons. In those cases, it does not make sense to carry on with the project.

2. Populate the Slotting Database

Slotting is data-intensive. Without comprehensive and accurate data describing the activity, dimensions, and storage characteristics of the items in the warehouse, intelligent slotting is impossible. Fortunately, the number of data elements required for slotting is not overwhelming. An example list of data requirements follows. For each item, we need the

- Item number
- Item description
- Material type
- Storage environment (frozen, refrigerated, flammable, hazardous, and so on)
- Shelf life
- Dimensions (L, W, H)
- Item unit cube
- Weight
- Units per carton
- Cartons per pallet
- Base unit of measure

This information should be readily available from the product or item master file. Just the process of evaluating the accuracy and availability of this data is helpful as a data integrity audit.

For each customer order, we need the

- Customer identification
- Unique items requested on the order and the quantities of each
- Order date and time

This information should be available from the sales and/or order history file. The sample size required depends heavily on the seasonality of the industry. If large annual surges of demand occur, such as in the mail order and retailing industries, then a 12-month sample is necessary. If the demand is fairly stable over the course of a year, as in automotive service parts, then a three- to six-month sample will be appropriate.

3. Compute Slotting Statistics

Once the raw data is captured, the computation of the slotting statistics is fairly straightforward. Unfortunately, the natural interpretations and application of the results may be counterintuitive and misleading. The family of slotting statistics computable from the slotting database is shown in Table 8-4.

These statistics appear on the surface to be self-explanatory. However, some subtle but critical issues surround the interpretation of each statistic. For example, popularity is often incorrectly measured in sales dollars or unit sales. The *popularity* (P) of an item, like the popularity of a song on a jukebox, should be measured by the number of times it is requested. This indicator is critical because it is a measure of the number of potential times an operator will visit the location for a particular item. Because most of the work in a warehouse is traveling to, from, and between warehouse locations, knowledge of the potential location visits for individuals and families of items is critical to success in managing the overall work content in the warehouse.

Unfortunately, many warehouse managers and analysts stop with popularity in their search for slotting criteria. Popularity is used singly to assign items to storage modes, to allocate space in storage modes, and to locate items within storage modes. Let's consider the example of golden zoning a section of bin shelving. The objective is to maximize the amount of picking activity that is done at or near waist level. Assume there is seven cubic feet of space

TABLE 8-4   **Slotting Statistics, Symbols, and Units of Measure**

Slotting Statistic	Symbol	Unit(s) of Measure	Notes and Comments
Slotting period	R	Time (year, quarter, month, week, day)	The time period for slotting calculations.
Popularity	P	Requests per period	Sometimes referred to as the hits on an item. Used with volume to determine an assignment to a storage mode and location within the storage mode.
Turnover	T	Units shipped per period	Sometimes referred to as the demand for an item. Used with unit cube to compute cube movement for storage mode assignment and space allocation.
Unit cube	C	Ft^3/unit	Measures the physical size of one unit of a unique item. The information may already be in a database. If not, C can be computed by measuring the size of the outer container for the item (pallet, case, tote, or bag) and dividing by the number of units in the container.
Cube movement	$V = T \times C$	Ft^3/Period	Sometimes referred to as the volume. Used to determine the appropriate storage mode and the allocation of space in the storage mode.
Pick density	$D = P/V$	Requests/Ft^3	Used in golden zoning. The items with the highest pick density should be assigned to the most accessible picking locations.
Demand increment	$I = T/P$	Units per request	
Standard deviation of demand	S		Measure of the daily standard deviation of demand.

TABLE 8-5   Slotting Example

Item ID	Popularity	Cube-Movement	Pick Density
A	140 requests/month	7 ft³/month	20 requests/ft³
B	108 requests/month	4 ft³/month	27 requests/ft³
C	75 requests/month	3 ft³/month	25 requests/ft³

available in the golden zone. Suppose we are considering three times for slotting. The slotting statistics for the three items are recorded in Table 8-5 .

Suppose we decide to store a month's supply of material in bin shelving. Item A requires seven cubic feet, item B requires four cubic feet, and item C requires three cubic feet. Suppose we rank the items based on popularity alone to determine the order of preference for assignment into the golden zone. (Remember the golden zone only has seven cubic feet of capacity.) With the popularity ranking, item A will be assigned to (and will exhaust the available space in) the golden zone. There will be 140 visits to the golden zone per month. (Remember we are trying to maximize the number of trips to the golden zone.) Is that the best we can do? Absolutely not! Suppose we assign items B and C to the golden zone. In that case, there will be 183 trips to the golden zone. Had we used pick density as the criteria for the preference ranking, we would have maximized the activity in the golden zone. That is why that measure of picking activity is so critical to the success of slotting and is consequently why it is so important to have all of the slotting statistics available.

4. Construct the Warehouse Activity Profile

The slotting statistics and order files should be used to develop a full warehouse activity profile. The composition of a warehouse activity profile was fully explained in Chapter 2, "Warehouse Activity Profiling." With those profiles in hand, the next step is to define item families for family slotting. Two profiles that were not explained in Chapter 2 that are critical for slotting are the storage mode profile and the operations planning profile. The picking mode profile defines the picking modes that are being considered. An example picking mode profile for broken case picking systems is presented in Table 8-6.

An operations planning profile defines the design and economic analysis parameters upon which operation design decisions, including slotting,

TABLE 8-6   **Example Picking Mode Profile**

	Bin Shelving	Flow Rack	Storage Drawers	Horizontal Carousels	Vertical Carousels	Miniload AS/RS	Automated Dispensing
Pick rate (lines per person-hour)	90	70	50	150	80	60	1,200
Restocking rate (restocks per person-hour)	45	60	30	40	35	35	400
Time supply (days)	20	5	20	10	20	20	20
Picking accuracy	0.95	0.95	0.95	0.95	0.95	0.95	0.95
Net investment cost ($/CF)	$15.00	$30.00	$40.00	$50.00	$75.00	$65.00	$300.00
PTL display cost per SKU	$200.00	$200.00	$120.00	$40.00	$60.00	n/a	n/a
Footprint density (CF/SF)	1.17	0.5	2	1.2	6	4	1.2

will be based. An example of an operations planning profile is presented in Table 8-7.

5. Assign Items to Item Families

Guided by the warehouse activity profiles, the next step is to assign items to item families. The process is a progressive sifting process (see Figure 8-14). The steps of the sifting process are outlined here.

a.   Assign items to *storage environment families* based on the requirements for storage temperature (frozen, refrigerated, and ambient), flammability, and/or hazardous storage. These storage environment families will specify the need for special building requirements, special racking requirements, and special material handling zones.

b.   Within each storage environment, assign items to *order completion zones* based on the order completion and demand correlation analysis completed in warehouse activity profiling. These order completion zones will create warehouses within the warehouse for highly efficient order picking.

TABLE 8-7   Example Operations Planning Profile

Planning Criteria	Value	Unit of Measure
Wage rate	$ 11	Dollars per hour
Occupancy cost	$ 5	Dollars per square foot per year
Planning horizon	5	Years
Working days per year	250	Days
Working hours per day	12	Hours per day
Error cost	$ 30	Dollars per error

FIGURE 8-14   Slotting decision tree.

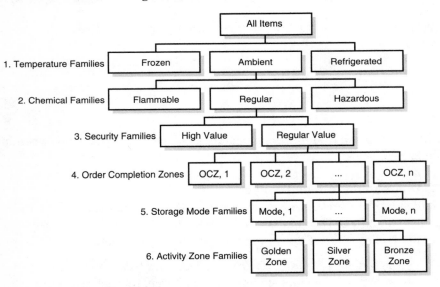

c.   Within each storage environment, within each order completion zone, assign items to *item activity families* based on cube movement, popularity, and pick density families. These families will be the basis for assigning items to storage modes, allocating space within storage modes, and assigning specific locations within the storage modes.

6. Assign Item Activity Families to Storage Mode Families

Based on productivity, storage density, picking error rates, and system investment requirements, a storage mode economic analysis should determine the least cost storage mode for each item. The items assigned to a particular storage mode become the members of that storage mode's family. LRI's slotting optimization tools compute the annualized cost of assigning each item to each storage mode. The least cost mode is recommended for each item. Examples in Figures 8-15 and 8-16 illustrate the assignment of item activity families to storage mode families.

7. Map the Individual Warehouse Locations Within Each Storage Mode into Picking Activity Zones

The first step in this mapping is to plot the pick path through each storage mode. Once the pick path through the pick line has been determined, the definition of the activity zones is fairly straightforward. The two most popular pick paths are the serpentine pick path and the mainline path with side trips (see Figure 8-17).

In *serpentine picking*, the order picker will by definition travel down each aisle and by each location. Hence, designating an A activity zone near one end of the pick line will not reduce travel time. In fact, it may create

FIGURE 8-15   Storage mode optimization for small items.

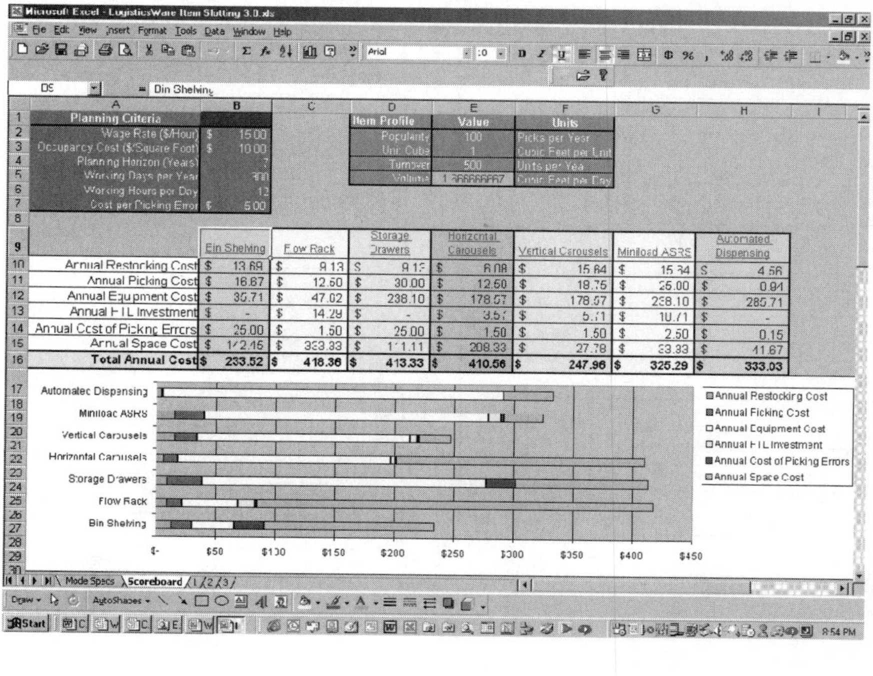

FIGURE 8-16 Storage mode optimization for pallet storage.

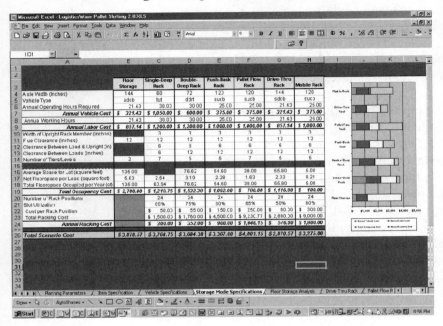

FIGURE 8-17 Serpentine picking and mainline picking with side trips.

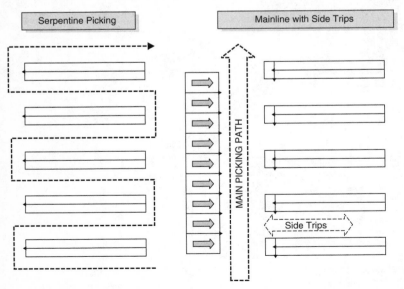

congestion problems. Instead, the A activity zone should be defined as the locations that are at or near waist level for broken case picking, and at or near floor level for case picking from pallet rack.

In *mainline picking with side trips*, the objective is to minimize the number and length of the side trips. Hence, the A activity zone should be defined as the locations along the mainline.

In *order picking from a pod of two or three carousels*, picking from alternating carousels should eliminate any idle time for the order picker waiting on the carousel, and the A activity zone should be defined as the locations at or near waist level. A mapping of storage mode locations into activity zones is illustrated in Figure 8-18.

8. Based on Pick Density, Assign Items to Storage Mode Activity Zones
Beginning with the item that has the highest pick density (and in descending order of pick density), begin assigning items to the A activity zone, then the B zone, and finally the C zone until the list of items is exhausted. An example assignment of items to storage modes and pick zones is illustrated in Table 8-8.

FIGURE 8-18   **Mapping of storage mode locations into activity zones.**

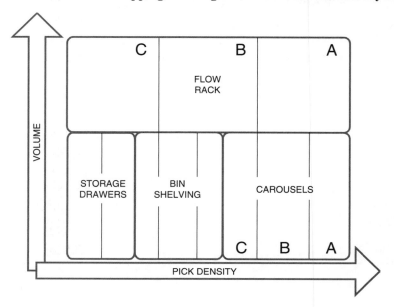

TABLE 8-8   Example Slotting Assignment Output

Item ID	Mode	Zone	Pick Face
013710	Horizontal carousels	A	0.929
307015	Horizontal carousels	A	8.258
306001	Horizontal carousels	A	8.323
307014	Horizontal carousels	A	20.457
018015	Horizontal carousels	B	0.692
322002	Horizontal carousels	B	1.213
245009	Horizontal carousels	B	1.243
328002	Horizontal carousels	B	1.915
322001	Horizontal carousels	B	2.883
244318	Horizontal carousels	C	0.461
322004	Horizontal carousels	C	0.609
375893	Horizontal carousels	C	0.878
307008	Horizontal carousels	C	0.924
323004	Horizontal carousels	C	1.878
319706	Horizontal carousels	C	2.446
326006	Horizontal carousels	C	3.506
307016	Flow rack	A	7.166
307002	Flow rack	A	8.008
081093	Flow rack	A	9.780
322008	Flow rack	A	9.899
307012	Flow rack	A	10.061
318001	Flow rack	A	10.828
245574	Flow rack	A	11.211
315002	Flow rack	A	11.448
011390	Flow rack	A	11.762
307013	Flow rack	A	11.951
330001	Flow rack	A	12.473
317001	Flow rack	A	70.468
015103	Flow rack	A	79.992
015409	Flow rack	A	82.628

9. Specify Reslotting Rules

Unfortunately, almost as soon as an item is properly slotted, its activity profile changes. For example, in the mail order industry, changes in catalogs yield major changes to the warehouse activity profile and major changes to the slotting requirements. Hence, it is critical to maintain a current slotting to maintain the productivity and storage density gains that are achieved under the initial slotting program.

Based on the initial slotting, reslotting rules should be defined to suggest when and if a particular item should be reslotted. The rules can be developed with the help of a simple from-to chart that computes the potential cost savings of moving an item from its current mode and zone to every other mode and zone. This savings is compared with the cost to move the item. If the savings-to-cost ratio exceeds a predetermined threshold, the item is recommended for reslotting. Note that a more convenient opportunity for reslotting an item occurs when its pick location inventory drops to zero. In that case, the slotting system should suggest the most appropriate slotting for the item and direct the restocking operator to the new location for the item. An example of a reslotting screen from a recent client engagement is provided in Figure 8-19. The tool prioritizes reslotting based on the number of activity zones by which an item is mis-slotted.

Perhaps a more difficult question is the timing of a general reslotting of the entire warehouse. Unfortunately, there is very little science to go on here. Most warehouses have a natural demand rhythm. For example, L.L. Bean, the mail order catalog operator, drops four main catalogs a year: Winter, Spring, Fall, and Summer. It is natural in that case to reslot the warehouse every season. In some operations, there is a slow period at the first of the year. That may be a perfect time to reslot the warehouse. Avon Products has 26 promotional campaigns a year. The warehouse has to be reslotted 26 times a year.

Lifeway Christian Resources

Lifeway Christian Resources publishes and distributes Christian media (books, periodicals, cassette tapes, CDs, and videosand gift items) to bookstores (retail distribution), churches (church distribution), and individuals (mail order) all over the United States. More than 15,000 items are housed in its 600,000-square-foot distribution center in downtown Nashville, Tennessee. The reserve inventory for each business unit is centralized and housed in high-bay, random locations. The forward, picking inventory is housed in dedicated locations on separate low-bay picking floors for each

FIGURE 8-19 Lifeway Christian Resources order picking layout.

Slotting Relocation Optimizer (by SKU)

SKU	ItemName	LocID	ZoneID	LocName	RecLocID	RecZoneID	RecLocName	ZoneChange
100001	expansion bay 4gb hd pbg3	460	4	B081011	815	2	B010523	2
100003	mhz 56kv90 pccardcombo w/xjack	1467	1	B010853	1762	4	B020252	-3
100011	li-ion battery 380/385	817	2	B010621	1125	3	B011131	-1
100107	averkey300 gold	707	1	B040743	1084	3	B050433	-2
100139	ephoto 1680	2044	4	B050213	1427	4	B030242	0
100144	3com10/100faste-linkpccard 5pk	1362	4	B050233	1603	2	B020653	2
100145	buz for powermac g3	132	2	B080643	546	1	B040722	1
100157	tview micro xga	1337	4	B030232	1679	3	B050353	1
100177	rapid access keyboard	932	2	B040542	1196	3	B041243	-1
100182	56kv90 xjack pcc modem	633	1	B021631	1023	3	B031222	-2
100196	clabs sound blaster livel	536	1	B030821	918	2	B051443	-1
100197	adobe illus 8 mac	41	1	B071632	44	1	B070732	0
100199	adobe /illus 8 upgd mac	10	1	B071621	8	1	B071522	0
10020	bjc600 magenta cartridge (bji-	1476	1	B011654	249	4	B070933	-3
10021	bjc600 cyan cartridge (bji-201	1421	4	B031042	1570	2	B041453	2
10022	bjc600 yellow cartridge (bji-	1448	4	B010944	1740	4	B031051	0
100241	naturally speak. v3.0 standard	1827	1	B040713	2098	4	B010212	-3
100336	quicken basic 99-win	502	1	B010722	187	3	B070331	-2
100345	filemaker pro 4.1 mac	18	1	B080823	69	1	B081543	0
100403	macopener v4.0	581	1	B061531	928	2	B041441	-1
100411	maclinkplus deluxe 10.1	34	1	B080831	62	1	B080742	0
100415	conflict catcher 8	16	1	B080821	28	1	B081631	0
100445	sonicwall firewall 10 nodes	1881	2	B050513	338	3	B070352	-1
100465	2.5" kanguru pcmcia kit	1701	4	B060951	1820	1	B031612	3
10047	just grandma & me cd	1049	3	B060321	1112	3	B021134	0

business unit. Because the business is a low-margin business, there is little or no capital available for highly mechanized systems. Hence, the design strategy is to eliminate and streamline as much work content as possible.

The slotting and layout plan for the retail picking floor is illustrated in Figure 8-20. Note the main, horseshoe pick line in the center of the warehouse. While traversing this pick line, order pickers pick approximately 20 orders per pass. A specially designed cart organized to hold 24 orders enables the pickers to quickly and efficiently sort individual picks into orders as they go. Items with the highest cube-movement are housed in carton flow rack in the center of the layout. Because each picking tour will pass each flow rack bay, the picking activity is purposefully distributed evenly along the flow rack pick line. The most popular flow rack items are located in the golden zone for the flow rack, the level of the flow rack at or near waist level. The remainder of the items falls naturally into bin shelving.

To minimize travel time, the bin shelving items with the greatest pick density are assigned to the locations along or near the pick line. This slotting scheme alleviates any congestion problems and allows nearly 75 per-

FIGURE 8-20 **Picking tour prior to pick sequencing.**

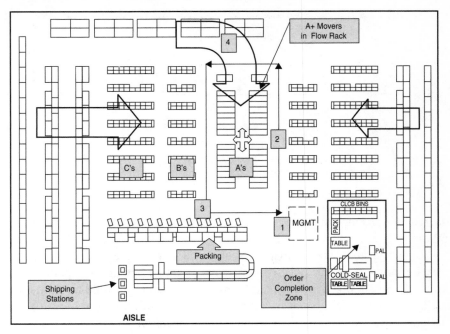

cent of the picks to be executed along the main pick line. The reserve stock for the gravity flow lanes is housed in double-deep pallet rack along the back wall. Batched replenishments are executed along the back of the flow lanes. Reserve stock for the bin shelving is conveniently located in single-deep pallet rack along the side walls.

This slotting and operating scheme yielded a 100-percent improvement in productivity and response time with minimal capital investment and risk.

8.7 PICK SEQUENCING

Sequence pick location visits to reduce travel time.

In both operator-to-stock and stock-to-operator systems, sequencing pick location visits can dramatically reduce travel time and increase picking productivity. For example, the travel time for a man-aboard AS/RS picking tour can be reduced by 50 percent by simply dividing the rack into upper and lower halves. Then you would visit pick locations in the lower half in increasing distance from the front of the rack on the outbound leg, and in

FIGURE 8-21   **Picking tour after pick sequencing.**

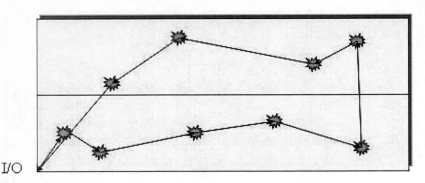

decreasing distance in the upper half on the rack during the inbound leg (see Figure 8-21).

Location visits should also be sequenced in walk-and-pick systems. In case picking operations, when an order may occupy one or more pallets, the picking tour should be sequenced to enable the picker to build a stable load and to reduce travel distance. A major distributor of photographic supplies uses an expert system to solve this complex problem.

C H A P T E R

9

UNITIZING AND SHIPPING

M ANY OF THE WORLD-CLASS receiving principles apply in reverse in shipping, including direct loading (the reverse of direct unloading), advanced shipping notice preparation (prereceiving), and staging in racks. To those we add the following practices in defining a world-class shipping activity:

- Container optimization
- Container loading and void fill
- Weigh checking
- Automated loading
- Dock management

9.1 CONTAINER OPTIMIZATION

Select cost and space-effective handling units.

The impact of the design and selection of shipping containers throughout the entire supply chain is one of the most neglected opportunities for increasing logistics efficiencies. Organizations rarely consider the excess costs and inefficiencies associated with missized, mislabeled, weak, and awkwardly configured containers. Because containers of all kinds—cartons, totes, pallets, trailers, 20- and 40-foot ocean containers, rail cars, and air containers—are the building blocks of the supply chain, the costs of the inefficiencies multiply across all supply chain partners. Containers should protect, secure, and identify the merchandise they contain (see Figure 9-1).

Containers should stack and nest easily, collapse when they are empty, handle comfortably, fit together naturally with other containers (see Figure 9-2), and provide an easy means for tracking and tracing.

Containers should be reusable and/or returnable to minimize the impact of logistics on the environment (see Figure 9-3).

Reusable and returnable containers help reduce the waste produced in any logistics system. Some examples of reusable and returnable containers are plastic pallets, plastic totes, collapsible roll cages, and multiuse corrugated containers.

The container design that minimizes the total life cycle cost of containerization, including the initial cost of the container, packaging costs, handling costs, space costs, container maintenance, product damage, and potential security losses, should be chosen and implemented.

FIGURE 9-1   Secure roll cages at one of Europe's largest shoe retailers minimize the likelihood of theft during loading, transit, or unloading.

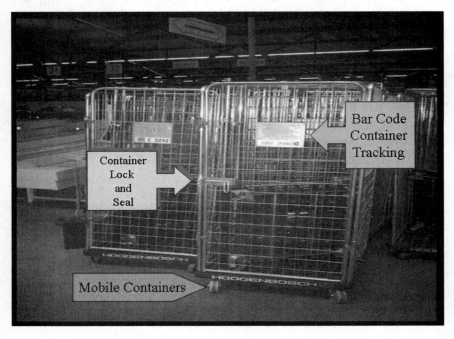

FIGURE 9-2   Modularity in container configurations.

FIGURE 9-3   Reusable and returnable containers.

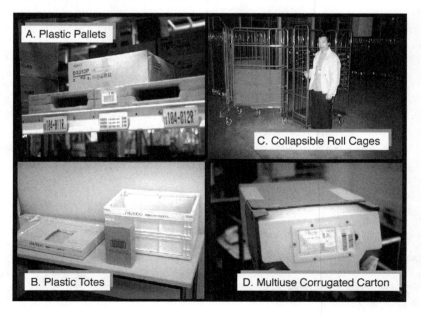

9.2   CONTAINER LOADING AND VOID FILL

Container load plans should be developed to maximize the cube and weight utilization of each container while balancing loading within the container and organizing product within the container to facilitate unloading. Advanced warehouse management systems suggest and illustrate optimal container loading plans (see Figure 9-4).

Environmentally friendly dunnage and void fill should be used to minimize product shifting and damage in-transit (see Figure 9-5). One example is recyclable and reusable air packs used as dunnage in Shiseido's order totes. Another example is the styrofoam pads used between pallet loads in KAO's trailer fleet. The last example is polystyrene peanuts. Some polystyrene peanuts are recyclable. In all cases, dunnage and void fill should be returnable or recyclable to avoid harmful effects on the environment.

9.3   WEIGH CHECKING

Outbound containers should be weighed and cubed for load-planning purposes. Weigh checking (see Figure 9-6) should be employed to identify any picking or packing errors before product loading.

9.4   AUTOMATED, DIRECT LOADING

Eliminate shipping staging and direct load outbound trailers.

As was the case in receiving, the most space and labor-intensive activity in shipping is staging activity. To facilitate the direct loading of pallets onto outbound trailers, pallet jacks and counterbalance lift trucks can serve as picking and loading vehicles, allowing a bypassing of staging. To go one step further, automating pallet loading can be accomplished using pallet conveyor interfacing with specially designed trailer beds to enable pallets to be automatically conveyed onto outbound trailers, with automated fork trucks, and/or automated guided vehicles (see Figure 9-7). Direct, automated loading of loose cases is facilitated with an extendable conveyor.

FIGURE 9-4   **Example of container load plan.**
Source: Loadlogic

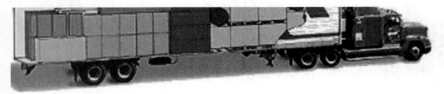

FIGURE 9-5   Dunnage and void fill should be used inside containers to minimize in-transit product damage by reducing and cushioning shifting.

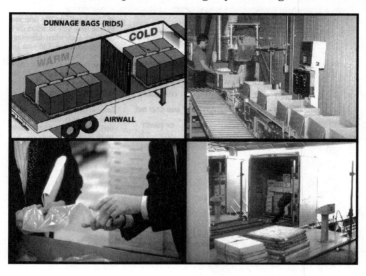

FIGURE 9-6   Weigh checking.

9.5   DOCK MANAGEMENT

Automate and optimize dock assignments and route on-site drivers through the site with minimum paperwork and in the most time-efficient manner.

FIGURE 9-7   Automated, direct vehicle loading.

FIGURE 9-8   Dock door assignment.

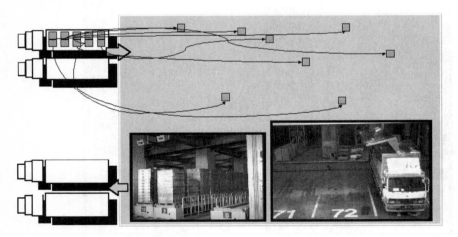

A variety of systems are now in place to improve the management of shipping and receiving docks and trailer drivers. Inbound trailers should be assigned to the dock closest to the centroid of the putaway locations on board (see Figure 9-8). Outbound trailers should be assigned to the dock door closest to the contents of the load it will pick up.

C H A P T E R 10

WAREHOUSE LAYOUT

THE PROCESS OF LAYING OUT a warehouse is a lot like putting a puzzle together. Like a puzzle, it is difficult to complete until all the pieces have been defined and assembled. Defining those pieces is the purpose of profiling, benchmarking, simplifying, computerizing, and mechanizing warehouse operations. In these five steps, we work to define individual processes and the types of material handling and storage systems working inside the warehouse. Putting those processes and systems together in an efficient and flexible building layout is the subject of this chapter.

Our five-step methodology for warehouse layout is presented in the following. The methodology requires as input the warehouse activity profile, the performance goals for the operation, the definition and configuration of the warehouse processes, and the configuration of all material handling and storage systems.

10.1 SPACE REQUIREMENTS PLANNING: DETERMINE THE OVERALL SPACE REQUIREMENTS FOR ALL WAREHOUSE PROCESSES

A warehouse layout should be based on the space requirements for and the interrelationships between individual warehouse processes. The first step in laying out a warehouse is to determine the overall space requirements for all warehouse processes. The space requirements for each process should be computed and summarized to estimate the overall building requirements. An example format for recording and summarizing the space requirements for a warehouse is provided in Table 10-1.

TABLE 10-1   Warehouse Space Requirements Worksheet

Process	Floorspace Requirements (Square Feet)	Notes and Comments
1. Receiving staging	30,000	Assuming 80% utilization.
2. Pallet storage	120,000	At peak inventory.
3. Case picking	25,000	
4. Broken case picking	15,000	
5. Packing & unitizing	15,000	
6. Customizing	20,000	Assumes 10% growth in VAS.
7. Accumulation & sortation	30,000	
8. Shipping staging	30,000	
9. Cross-docking	15,000	
10. Warehouse offices	15,000	
11. Restrooms	5,000	
Subtotal	320,000	
Interactivity aisle allowance	64,000	@ 20% of subtotal.
TOTAL	**384,000**	

Receiving and shipping staging space is a function of the number of receiving and shipping dock doors and the turnaround time for each dock. A common practice is to allocate enough staging space behind each dock door to accommodate a truckload's worth of material.

Floorspace requirements for pallet storage and retrieval, case picking, and broken case picking should be computed as part of the storage mode economic analysis (see Chapter 5, "Pallet Storage and Retrieval Systems," and Chapter 7, "Small Item Picking Systems"). One of the most difficult decisions to make in storage space planning is the portion of the peak storage requirement to accommodate. If the duration of the peak is short-lived and the ratio of the peak to average ratio is high, then temporary space (outside warehousing and/or trailer storage) should be considered to accommodate the peak storage requirements (see Figure 10-1). If the duration of the peak is for an extended period and the ratio of the peak to average ratio is low, then the warehouse should be sized at or very near peak requirements (see Figure 10-2).

FIGURE 10-1   Storage capacity requirements over time with high peak to average ratio.

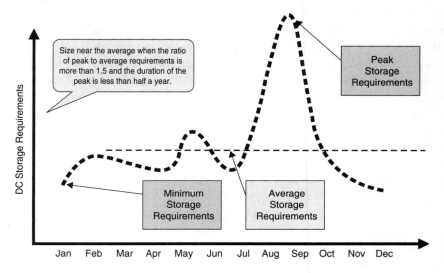

FIGURE 10-2   Storage capacity requirements over time with low peak to average ratio.

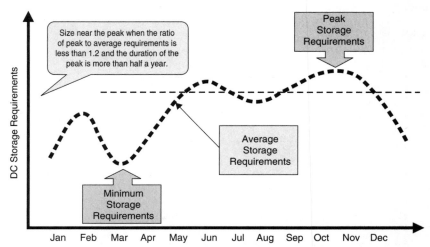

Another important consideration in storage space requirements planning is the portion of warehouse locations that will be occupied for planning purposes. As the utilization of storage locations exceeds 85 percent in nonreal-time warehouses and 90 percent in real-time warehouses, the productivity and safety of the operations trail off dramatically (see Figure 10-3).

Floorspace requirements for packing, unitizing, customizing, accumulation, and sortation are computed as a function of the floorspace required for each work station in those areas, the number of work stations required, and the material handling methods employed in each area.

Warehouse office space is simply a function of the number of offices and the floorspace required for each. The floorspace required for restrooms can be computed from local building code requirements.

The sum of the floorspace requirements for each process is a subtotal to which an interprocess aisle allowance is added to yield total floorspace requirements. The following case example illustrates a high-level warehouse sizing and floorspace requirements estimation exercise.

Heavy Machinery Inc. (HMI)

I was asked on a recent project to plan the aggregate warehousing space requirements for HMI for the next five years. Because pallet storage is the most space intensive process in a warehouse, I began by computing the stor-

FIGURE 10-3   **Warehouse productivity versus warehouse location occupancy.**

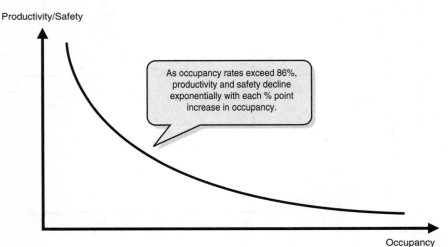

age space requirements for pallets. The computations are described in the following and summarized in Table 10-2 (In this simple analysis, I used data gathered in the warehouse activity profile to project the floorspace requirement for pallet storage.)

1. Divide forecasted unit sales (from marketing projections) by annual inventory turns (from material management) to compute the average unit inventory.

2. Divide the average unit inventory by the average units per pallet (from the item master file) to compute the average pallet inventory.

3. Multiply the average pallet inventory by the ratio of *peak-to-average* (PTA) inventory (from the item master file) to compute the peak pallet inventory.

4. Multiply the peak pallet inventory by the portion of peak inventory used for storage planning purposes to compute the effective pallet storage capacity.

5. Divide the effective pallet storage capacity by the location utilization factor (typically 85 percent for single-deep pallet storage) to compute the required number of pallet storage locations.

6. Divide the required number of pallet storage locations by the storage density (square feet per pallet computed as a function of the aisle width and storage height) to compute floorspace requirements.

Floorspace requirements in a given area and in the overall layout can and should be reduced by

- Running storage lanes and racking parallel to the long axis of the building

TABLE 10-2   Example Pallet Floorspace Requirements Computations

Year	Forecasted Usage	Projected Turns	Average Inventory	Average Pallets	Peak to Average Inventory Ratio	% of Peak for Planning	Maximum Location Utilization	Required Pallet Locations	Aisle Width	Storage Levels	Storage Density	Floorspace Requirement
2000	275,629	12	22,969	577	1.08	0.93	85%	681	9	3	24	16,354
2001	370,130	12	30,844	774	1.08	0.93	85%	915	9	3	24	21,961
2002	370,250	12	30,854	775	1.08	0.93	85%	915	9	3	24	21,969
2003	416,770	12	34,731	872	1.08	0.93	85%	1030	9	3	24	24,729
2004	465,545	12	38,795	974	1.08	0.93	85%	1151	9	3	24	27,623
2005	485,200	12	40,433	1015	1.08	0.93	85%	1200	9	3	24	28,789

FIGURE 10-4   Over-aisle storage.

Over-Aisle Storage

- Implementing a random storage location policy in large storage areas
- Utilizing over-aisle (see Figure 10-4) and over-dock storage (see Figure 10-5) when feasible
- Burying building columns in storage racks
- Running storage lanes and racking along interior walls

10.2   MATERIAL FLOW PLANNING: SPECIFY A U-SHAPE, STRAIGHT-THRU, OR MODULAR OVERALL FLOW DESIGN

In flow planning, we specify a U-shape, straight-thru, modular-spine, or multistory flow pattern.

U-Shaped Flow

An example U-shape warehouse flow design is illustrated in Figure 10-6. In the classic case, products flow in at receiving, move into storage in the back of the warehouse, and then to shipping, which is located adjacent to receiving on the same side of the building.

FIGURE 10-5   Over-dock and over-conveyorstorage.

FIGURE 10-6   Typical U-shaped flow pattern.

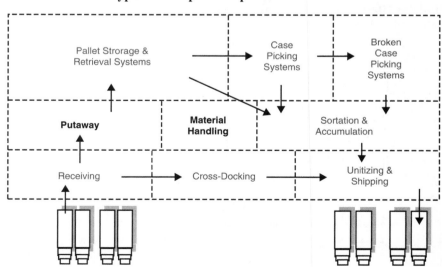

A U-shape flow design has a number of advantages over other flow designs including

- Excellent utilization of dock resources (dock doors, dock equipment, dock space, dock operators, and dock supervisors) because the receiving and shipping processes can share dock doors
- Facilitating cross-docking because the receiving and shipping docks are adjacent to one another and may be co-mingled
- Excellent lift truck utilization because putaway and retrieval trips are easily combined and because the storage locations closest to the receiving and shipping docks are natural locations to house fast moving items
- Enables expansion opportunities in three directions
- Yields excellent security because there is a single side of the building used for entry and exit

With these inherent advantages, the U-shape flow design is the benchmark upon which all other flow designs should be compared.

Straight-Thru Flow
Example straight-thru flow designs are illustrated in Figures 10-7 and 10-8. The straight-thru configuration lends itself to operations that are pure cross-

FIGURE 10-7 Straight-thru flow design.
Source: Bruce A. Strahan

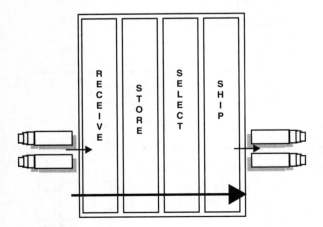

FIGURE 10-8   Straight-thru flow design for a grocery flow-thru operation.
Source: Bruce A. Strahan

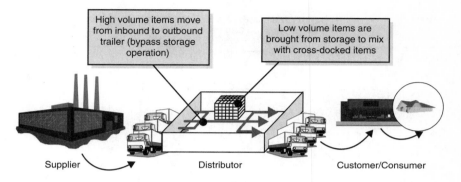

docking facilities (sometimes referred to as flow-through facilities) or operations in which the peak receiving and shipping times coincide. The major disadvantage is that the design makes it difficult to take advantage of ABC storage and dual command trips.

Modular-Spine Design

An example modular flow design is illustrated in Figure 10-9. Modular flow design is well suited for large-scale operations in which individual processes are so large they merit stand-alone and uniquely designed buildings. Examples include rack-supported buildings for a unit load AS/RS, an air conditioned low bay building for customizing operations such as monogramming, pricing, and marking; or a low-bay shipping building equipped with high-speed sortation equipment.

Figure 10-9 depicts a modular DC spine design for a large grocery distribution operation. The modules are dedicated to specific order flows and/or item popularity designations. For example, one module is dedicated to cross-docking transactions on A+ items, one to continuous flow transactions on A/B items, regular flows for B/C items, and slow flows on C/D items.

FIGURE 10-9   **An example of modular flow design with modules designed specifically for cross-docking (low-bay), continuous replenishment (medium bay), and medium and slow-moving items (high-bay).**

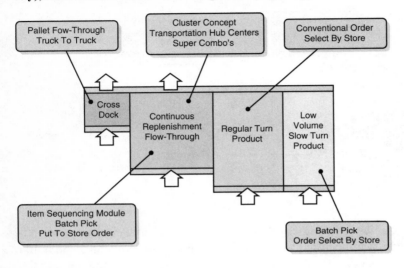

Multistory Layouts

Multistory distribution buildings (Figure 10-10) are necessary when land is extremely scarce. Multistory DCs are common in Japan and in some parts of Europe. They are the least desirable of the flow path alternatives because of the material handling difficulties and bottlenecks encountered in moving merchandise between floors.

10.3   ADJACENCY PLANNING: LOCATE FUNCTIONS WITH HIGH ADJACENCY REQUIREMENTS CLOSE TO ONE ANOTHER

Based primarily on material flow patterns, processes with high adjacency requirements should be located close to one another. For example, reserve storage should be located near receiving because there is typically a lot of material flow between receiving and reserve storage. The same can be said for receiving and cross-docking, cross-docking and shipping, case picking and pallet storage, case picking and broken case picking, picking activities and customizing and unitizing activities, and customizing and unitizing activities with shipping. These natural flow relationships often lead to the U-shape flow design illustrated in Figure 10-6.

FIGURE 10-10   Multistory warehouse designs.

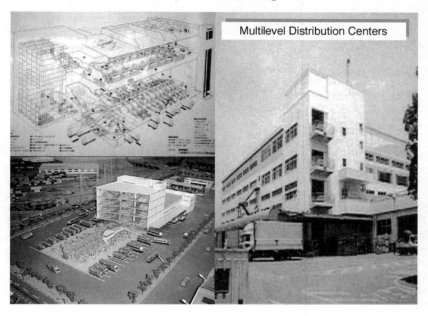

A warehouse activity relationship chart is used to document the adjacency requirements of the processes in a warehouse. Figures 10-11 and 10-12 give examples of warehouse activity relationship charts. Computer-aided facility layout tools such as CRAFT, CORELAP, and ALDEP take these adjacency requirements, the floorspace requirements of each process, and the location of fixed objects as inputs and compute an optimal block layout for a facility. These tools are initiated with the location of fixed elements including columns, exit doors, dock doors, railroad tracks, highways, and so on, so that processes may be oriented toward or away from them as necessary.

10.4   PROCESS LOCATION: ASSIGN PROCESSES WITH HIGH STORAGE REQUIREMENTS TO HIGH-BAY SPACE, AND LABOR INTENSIVE PROCESSES IN LOW BAY SPACE

One of the major reasons for low space utilization in warehouse facilities is that processes that can be executed in low-bay space—receiving, broken case picking, customization, returns processing, and so on—are often executed in high-bay space. If the high-bay space is existing, it can be mezzanined to

FIGURE 10-11   Warehouse activity relationship chart.

Source: Naval Supply Systems Command

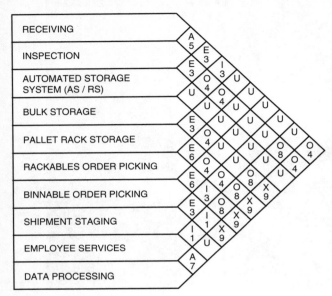

REASONS FOR IMPORTANCE

1. Supervision
2. Safety
3. Material flow
4. Work flow
5. Material control
6. Equipment proximity
7. Shared spaced
8. Employee health and safety
9. Security

PROXIMITY IMPORTANCE

A. Absolutely necessary
E. Especially important
I. Important
O. Ordinary closeness
U. Unimportant
X. Undesirable

accommodate multiple low-bay processes in the same floorspace. The key design principle is to assign processes with high storage requirements to high-bay space and labor intensive processes to low-bay space.

10.5   EXPANSION/CONTRACTION PLANNING: DOCUMENT EXPANSION AND CONTRACTION STRATEGIES FOR EACH WAREHOUSE PROCESS

The only thing we know about tomorrow is that it will be different from today. In a warehouse, different may mean larger or smaller, faster or slower, more variety or less variety, taller or shorter, more people or fewer people,

FIGURE 10-12 Activity relationship diagram (heavy lines indicate high adjacency requirements).

Source: Naval Supply Systems Command

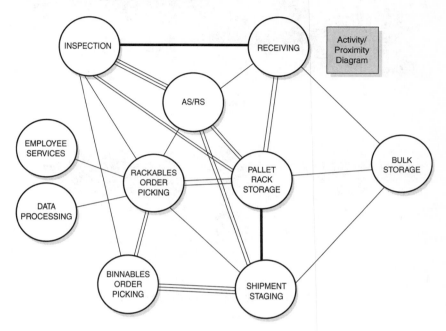

more technology or less technology, and so on. To accommodate the rapid pace of change, a carefully configured warehouse layout includes expansion and contraction plans for each area in the warehouse and for the warehouse as a whole. An example warehouse expansion plan is illustrated in Figure 10-13.

10.6   SUMMARY

Use the following principles as a checklist to insure that your warehouse layout meets world-class standards.

1. Determine the overall space requirements for all warehouse processes.

2. Specify a U-shape, straight-thru, or modular overall flow design.

3. Locate functions with high adjacency requirements close to one another.

FIGURE 10-13   Warehouse expansion concepts.
Source: Naval Supply Systems Command

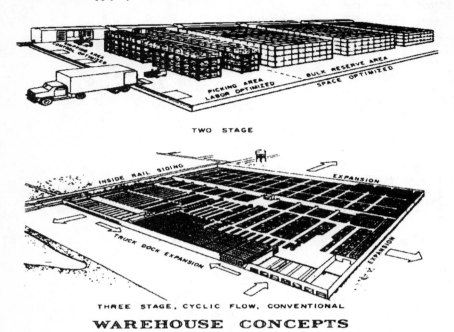

TWO STAGE

THREE STAGE, CYCLIC FLOW, CONVENTIONAL

WAREHOUSE CONCEPTS

4.   Assign processes with high storage requirements to high-bay space and labor intensive processes in low-bay space.

5.   Document expansion and contraction strategies for each warehouse process.

CHAPTER 11

COMPUTERIZING WAREHOUSE OPERATIONS

THE PROPER ROLE FOR the computer in warehouse operations is to help warehouse managers manage and to help warehouse operators operate. For managers, the computer should

- Continuously profile warehouse activity to help managers pinpoint and anticipate problem areas and major shifts in activity levels and patterns

- Continuously monitor warehouse performance in productivity, shipping and inventory accuracy, warehouse order cycle time, and storage density

- Continuously simplify the warehouse operations by reliably optimizing and communicating transactions to/from warehouse operators and equipment

For warehouse operators, the WMS should facilitate hands-free and paperless activities. It is that simple. If the WMS does not help the warehouse manager manage and the warehouse operators operate, what good is it? With over 400 providers of warehouse management systems aggressively marketing their products and in-house MIS groups eagerly encouraging system improvements, it is easy to lose sight of the fundamental improvements that computerizing warehouse operations should bring.

This chapter is not meant to be an exhaustive description of warehouse management system functions, features, strategies, and supplier alternatives. That's a book, not a chapter. In addition, warehouse management systems are not my area of expertise. Leveraging the capabilities of warehouse management systems, however, is my expertise, and it is critical to achieving world-class warehousing. In fact, I believe it is so critical to success in warehousing that the sequel to this book is already in the works and it is titled, *Computer-Aided Warehousing*.

Because the focus of this book is operational excellence, I have targeted two aspects of computerized warehousing that can make or break the operations. The first section of the chapter is a review of paperless warehousing devices and systems. Paperless warehousing devices are the interface between warehouse operators and the warehouse management system. Hence, the design and selection of these devices and systems is critical to the success of the overall operation. The second section of the chapter is a collection of recommendations on selecting, justifying, and implementing warehouse management systems. I have witnessed this process take a warehouse ahead ten years and set it behind by ten years.

11.1 PAPERLESS AND WIRELESS WAREHOUSE SYSTEMS

A full information technology solution for warehouse operations includes

- A computing platform (that is, mainframe, mid-range, client-server network, and/or network of personal computers)
- A network of paperless devices (that is, radio frequency terminals, bar code scanners, light-directed systems, and voice headsets)
- A relational and/or object database (that is, Oracle, Sybase, Informix, and/or proprietary)
- Warehouse management software
- Enterprise system interface software
- Material handling and paperless device interface software

Because there is already extensive material published on computing platforms, relational and object-oriented databases, and warehouse management software, this chapter focuses on paperless warehousing systems.

Paperless Warehousing Systems

Each year we conduct a survey to determine industry priorities for warehouse management systems functionality. Nearly every year the top three priorities are (1) paperless communications, (2) live inventory, and (3) productivity tracking.

Why is "paperless" the top priority? Many of the potholes on the road to world-class warehousing are related to paper and paper handling. First, it is easy to lose paper. I do it every day. Second, you have to read paper. Reading warehouse documents usually requires searching through a maze of information for just a single line that matters for the transaction at hand. As a result, transpositions can occur. Third, you have to write on paper. Again, it is easy to transpose something. Fourth, things on paper cannot be communicated in real time. As a result, errors in inventory levels and/or order status are never known. It is difficult to perform cross-docking and transaction interleaving without real-time systems. Fifth, paper is expensive to print, handle, and file. Sixth, it is easy to damage and smudge paper. Paperless warehousing and world-class warehousing go hand in hand.

Digital and real-time warehousing requires an enabling set of devices and technologies. These devices are the data collection and communication devices forming the backbone of integrated logistics information systems. Because the list of devices grows daily, it is impossible to present a current picture of the state of paperless logistics technologies in textbook form. Logistics industry trade shows and related Web sites are the best and perhaps only continually updated presentation of the current state of paperless logistics technologies.

Though the set of devices is changing and being upgraded rapidly, the general categories of technologies have remained fairly stable over the last few years. To support paperless logistics we need a way to automatically *identify* a logistics object (that is, a container, document, or location), a way to *communicate* information to a logistics operator, and a way to *present* information to a logistics operator. Those major categories of technologies are described and illustrated in this section:

- Automatic identification technologies
  - Bar codes and bar code scanners
  - Radio frequency tags and antennae
  - Smart cards and magnetic stripes
  - Vision systems
- Automatic communication and presentation technologies
  - Radio frequency data communications
  - Synthesized voice
  - Virtual displays
  - Pick-to-light systems

Automatic Identification Technologies

Bar Codes and Bar Code Scanners   A *bar code system* includes a bar code *symbology* to represent a series of alphanumeric characters, bar code *readers* to interpret the bar code symbology, and bar code *printers* to reliably and accurately print bar codes on labels, cartons, and/or picking/shipping documents. The review is included here because bar code systems are the foundation of many paperless warehousing systems, but the review is meant only as a brief introduction to bar code systems.

Bar Code Symbologies   A bar code (see Figure 11-1) is a series of printed bars and intervening spaces. The structure of unique bar/space patterns represents various alphanumeric characters. The same pattern may represent different alphanumeric characters in different codes.

The primary codes or symbologies for which standards have been developed include

- **Code 39**   An alpha-numeric code adopted by a wide number of industry and government organizations for both individual product identification and shipping package/container identification.
- **Interleaved 2 of 5 Code**   A compact, numeric-only code still used in a number of applications where alpha-numeric encoding is not required.
- **Universal Product Code (UPC)**   Used to record the unique product identifier on retail products.
- **Codabar**   One of the earlier symbols developed, this symbol permits encoding of the numeric-character set, six unique control characters and four unique stop/start characters that can be used to distinguish different item classifications. It is primarily used in nongrocery retail point of sale applications, blood banks, and libraries.

FIGURE 11-1   Linear bar code.

- **Code 93**   Accommodating all 128 ASCII characters plus 43 alpha-numeric characters and four control characters, Code 93 offers the highest alpha-numeric data density of the six standard symbologies. In addition to enabling for positive switching between ASCII and alpha-numeric, the code uses two check characters to ensure data integrity.

- **Code 128**   Provides the architecture for high density encoding of the full 128 character ASCII set, variable length fields and elaborate character-by-character, and full symbol integrity checking. Provides the highest numeric-only data density. Adopted in 1989 by the Uniform Code Council (U.S.) and the International Article Number Association (EAN) for shipping container identification.

- **UPC/EAN**   The numeric-only symbols developed for grocery supermarket point-of-sale applications and now widely used in a variety of other retailing environments. Fixed length code suitable for unique manufacturer and item identification only.

- **Stacked Symbologies**   Although a consensus standard has not yet emerged, the health and electronics industries have initiated programs to evaluate the feasibility of using Code 16K or Code 49, two micro-symbologies that offer significant potential for small item encoding. Packing data in from 2 to 16 stacked rows, Code 16K accommodates the full 128-character ASCII set and permits the encoding of up to 77 characters in an area of less than .5 square inches. Comparable in terms of data density, Code 49 also handles the full ASCII character set. It encodes data in from two to eight rows and has a capacity of up to 49 alpha-numeric characters per symbol.

- **Two-Dimensional Codes**   Two-dimensional bar codes, sometimes referred to as high-density bar codes, are the latest development in a rapidly advancing field. Two-dimensional codes are overlapping linear bar codes, one horizontal and the other vertical in the same field. These codes permit the automatic encoding of nearly a printed page's worth of text in a square inch of page space. Examples include Code 49, Code 16k, PDF 417, Code One, Datamatrix, and UPS's Maxicode.

Bar codes can be and are used for

- Product identification
- Container identification
- Location identification
- Operator identification

- Equipment identification
- Document identification

The tendency is to get caught up in bar coding for the sake of bar coding, trying to bar code anything and everything. The key to success is to minimize the amount of bar coding required to achieve the automatic communications objectives of logistics. If there is too much bar coding and too much bar code scanning, the costs and time to print and scan all the codes can quickly negate potential productivity and accuracy benefits.

Bar Code Readers   Bar codes are read by both contact and noncontact scanners. Contact scanners must contact the bar code. They can be portable or stationary and typically come in the form of a wand or a light pen. The wand/pen is manually passed across the bar code. The scanner emits either white or infrared light from the wand/pen tip and reads the light pattern that is reflected from the bar code. This information is stored in solid-state memory for subsequent transmission to a computer.

Contact readers (see Figure 11-2) are excellent substitutes for keyboard or manual data entry. Alphanumeric information is processed at a rate of up to 50 inches per minute, and the error rate for a basic scanner connected to its decode is 1 in 1,000,000 reads. Light pen or wand scanners with decoder and interface cost around $700.

FIGURE 11-2   Light-pen bar code scanner.

FIGURE 11-3   Handheld laser scanner.
Source: Symbol Technologies

Noncontact readers may be handheld (see Figure 11-3) or stationary (see Figure 11-4) and include fixed-beam scanners, moving-beam scanners, and *charged couple device* (CCD) scanners. Noncontact scanners employ fixed-beam, moving beam, video camera, or raster scanning technology to take from one to several hundred looks at the code as it passes. Most bar code scanners read codes bidirectionally by virtue of sophisticated decoding electronics, which distinguish the unique start/stop codes peculiar to each symbology and decipher them accordingly. Further, the majority of scanner suppliers now provide equipment with an autodiscrimination feature that permits recognition, reading, and verification of multiple symbol formats with no internal or external adjustments. Finally, suppliers have introduced omnidirectional scanners (see Figure 11-5) for industrial applications that are capable of reading bar codes passing through a large viewfield at high speeds, regardless of the orientation of the bar code. These scanners are commonly used in high-speed sortation systems.

Fixed-beam readers use a stationary light source to scan a bar code. They depend on the motion of the object to be scanned to move past the beam.

FIGURE 11-4   Inline bar code scanner.
Source: Computer Identics

FIGURE 11-5   Omnidirectional bar code scanning.

Fixed-beam readers rely on consistent, accurate code placement on the moving object.

Radio Frequency Tags *Radio frequency* (RF) tags encode data on a chip encased in a tag. When a tag is within range of a special antenna, the chip is decoded and read by a tag reader (see Figure 11-6). RF tags can be programmable or permanently coded and can be read from up to 70 feet away.

Surface acoustical wave (SAW) tags are permanently coded and can be read only within a ten-foot range.

RF tags are often used for permanent identification of a container, where advantage can be taken of the tag's durability. RF tags are also attractive in harsh environments where printed codes may deteriorate and become illegible. A tag reader costs around $5,000. Nonprogrammable tags range in price from $1 to $50, programmable tags, from $5 to $75.

At a large textiles manufacturer, the contents of a truckload are encoded into a RF tag located in the windshield of the truck. The tag can be read by antennae placed at ten mile increments along the highway to enable a customer to watch the progress of its load and to prelocate the contents of the truckload. This technology facilitates cross-docking and direct (no-staging) putaway of truckload contents to primary and reserve picking locations.

Magnetic Stripes and Optical Cards Magnetic stripes commonly appear on the back of credit or bank cards. They are used to store a large quantity

FIGURE 11-6 **RF tag application in yard management.**

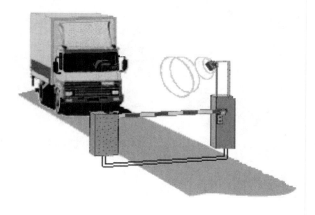

of information in a small space. The magnetic stripe is readable through dirt or grease. Data contained in the stripe can be changed. The stripe must be read by contact, thus eliminating high-speed sortation applications. Magnetic stripe systems are generally more expensive than bar code systems. In warehousing, magnetic stripes are used on smart cards in a variety of paperless applications. Smart cards are now used in logistics to capture information ranging from employee identification, to the contents of a trailer load of material (see Figure 11-7), to the composition of an order picking tour. For example, at a large cosmetics distribution center order picking tours are downloaded onto smart cards (see Figure 11-8). The smart cards are in turn inserted into a smart card reader built into each order picking cart. In so doing, the picking tour is illuminated on an electronic map of the warehouse appearing on the front of the cart.

Vision Systems   Vision system cameras take pictures of objects and codes and send the pictures to a computer for interpretation. Vision systems "read" at moderate speeds with excellent accuracy, at least for limited envi-

FIGURE 11-7   **Optical memory card used for automated truck manifesting and RF tag used in container identification.**

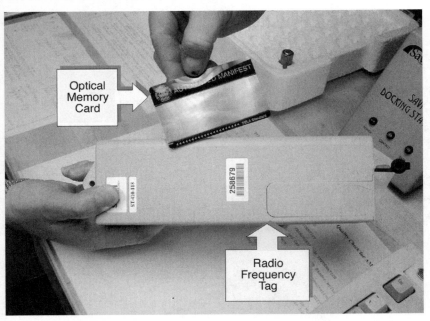

FIGURE 11-8   Smart cards in an order picking application.

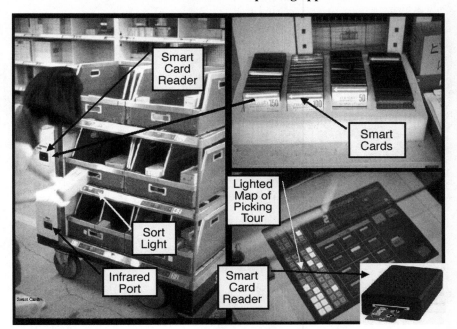

ronments. Obviously, these systems do not require contact with the object or code. However, the accuracy of a read is highly dependent on the quality of light. Vision systems are becoming less costly but are still relatively expensive.

A large mail order operator recently installed a vision system at receiving (see Figure 11-9). The system is located above a telescoping conveyor used to convey inbound cartons from a trailer into the warehouse. The system recognizes those inbound cartons that do not have bar codes, reads the product and vendor number on the carton, and directs a bar code printer to print and apply the appropriate bar code label.

Automatic Communication and Presentation Technologies

Radio Frequency Data Communications   Handheld, lift-truck mounted (see Figure 11-10), and hands-free *radio data terminals* (RDTs) (see Figure 11-11) are rapidly emerging as reliable tools for both inventory and vehicle/driver management. RDTs incorporate a multicharacter display, full

FIGURE 11-9   **Vision system used in automated receiving inspection.**
Source: Siemens

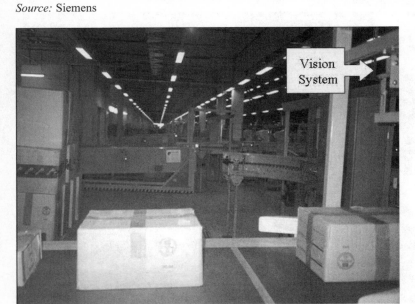

FIGURE 11-10   **Vehicle-mounted radio frequency terminals.**

FIGURE 11-11   Handsfree radio frequency terminals.
Source: Symbol Technologies

keyboard, and special function keys. They communicate and receive messages on a prescribed frequency via strategically located antennae and a host computer interface unit. Beyond the basic thrust toward tighter control of inventory, improved resource utilization is most often cited in justification of these devices. Further, the increasing availability of software packages that permit RDT linkage to existing plant or warehouse control systems greatly simplify their implementation. The majority of RDTs installed in plants and warehouses use handheld wands or scanners for data entry, product identification, and location verification. This marriage of technologies provides higher levels of speed, accuracy, and productivity than could be achieved by either technology alone.

Synthesized Voice   The use of synthesized voice (see Figure 11-12) is increasingly popular in warehouse operations. In stationary systems, a synthesized voice is used to direct a stationary warehouse operator. For example, at a wholesale grocery distribution center, carousel operators are directed by lights and a broadcast synthesized voice speaks the correct picking location and quantity.

FIGURE 11-12   Voice headset.
Source: Vocollect

In mobile voice-based systems, warehouse operators wear a headset with an attached microphone. Via synthesized voice, the WMS talks the operator through a series of transactions. For example, for a pallet putaway, the lift truck operator hears a command to put away a particular pallet into a particular warehouse location. When the transaction is complete, the operator speaks, "putaway complete" into the microphone. Then the system speaks the next transaction to the operator. If the operator forgets the transaction, he simply speaks, "repeat transaction" and the system repeats the instruction.

The advantages of voice-based systems include hands-free operations, the operator's eyes are free from terminals or displays, and the system functions whether or not the operator is literate. Another advantage is the ease with which the system is programmed. A simple Windows-based software package is used to construct all necessary transaction conversations. To operate every area of the warehouse with a voice-based system would require conversations for receiving, putaway, restocking, order picking, and shipping. Once those conversations have been developed, the system is a WMS unto itself. This approach can be an inexpensive way to achieve a majority of the functionality of a typical WMS. A typical mobile voice-based system costs approximately the same as a RDT-based system, in the range of $1,000 to $3,000 per terminal.

Virtual "Heads Up" Displays   Virtual (or "heads up") displays (see Figure 11-13) present an operator with virtual overlays on the warehouse floor, products, or layouts to direct an operator through travel paths and/or to perform specific transactions on specific products (see Figure 11-14). The displays can also be used to present the operator with a virtual computer display and or to take an operator on a virtual tour of a 3D warehouse layout. That application can be used in training warehouse operators in working the full range of warehouse transactions in each area within the warehouse.

Pick-to-Light Systems   Light-directed operations (see Figure 11-15) use indicator lights and lighted alphanumeric displays to direct warehouse operators in order picking, putaway, and/or sortation. The most popular use is in broken case picking from flow racks, shelving, and/or carousels. In the case of flow rack or bin shelving, a light display is placed at the front of each

FIGURE 11-13   **"Heads Up" warehouse display.**
Source: VRwarehouse.com

FIGURE 11-14   Virtual warehouse picking tour.
Source: VRwarehouse.com

FIGURE 11-15   Pick-to-light systems.

pick location (in the place of a location label). The light is illuminated if a pick is required from that location. The number of units to pick appears on the same display or on a display at the top of the flow rack or shelving bay. A typical light display system costs in the range of $100 to $200 per SKU position. Typical picking rates are in the range of 300 to 600 lines per person-hour and accuracy is in the range of 99.97 percent. In incremental justification, these rates and accuracies must pay for the incremental computer hardware and software costs.

In carousels, a light tree is placed in front of each carousel. A light display appears on the tree to correspond to every picking level on the carousel. As a carrier is positioned in front of the order picker, the light display corresponding to the level to be picked from is illuminated. A typical light tree for carousel picking costs in the range of $100,000. However, if we normalize the cost by the number of items on a typical carousel, say 5,000, then the cost per SKU position is only $20.

Lights can also be used to direct case picking and pallet storage and retrieval operations.

11.2   WAREHOUSE MANAGEMENT SYSTEM JUSTIFICATION, SELECTION, AND IMPLEMENTATION

The process of selecting, justifying, and implementing a *warehouse management system* (WMS) can raise a warehouse to world-class status or set the operation back ten years. Rarely is there anything in the middle. It is risky business for the business and for your career as well. Here's a little advice for your trip down this rocky road.

WMS Selection
The WMS selection process begins with the decision to build or buy the system. The pros and cons of building and buying warehouse management systems are summarized in Table 11-1.

If you decide to buy a system, remember that there are over 400 suppliers of WMS applications. Even the largest of these suppliers does less than $50 million per year in sales. Hence, all WMS vendors are by definition small companies. Selecting a supplier is treacherous business. This point registered with me loud and clear during a marketability assessment of a large supplier's WMS. The functional evaluation is illustrated in Figure 11-16. The technical evaluation is illustrated in Figure 11-17.

In this case, the functionality of the system is poor, yet the technical capability of the system is above average. Would you choose this system to

TABLE 11-1   WMS Buy Versus Build Decision Issues

Issue	Buy vs. Build	
Initial expense	Initial WMS expense is lower through large package suppliers because their development expense is leveraged against many clients.	
Maintenance expense		If the in-house staff is highly competent in WMS, then the in-house maintenance may be more timely and less expensive. Otherwise, a package supplier will be less expensive and perhaps the only feasible alternative.
Customization	The world's best warehouse management systems were all built in-house. Customization of world-class operating principles to unique industry settings is the key. If warehousing is a key to your competitiveness, customization is critical.	
Response to changes		If the in-house staff is highly competent in WMS, then the in-house changes will be more timely and less expensive. Otherwise, a package supplier will be less expensive and perhaps the only feasible alternative.
Influence of outside expertise		In either case, the WMS design should be influenced by someone(s) knowledgeable in world-class warehousing practices. Unfortunately, many WMS providers lack true warehousing expertise.

FIGURE 11-16   WMS functional evaluation.

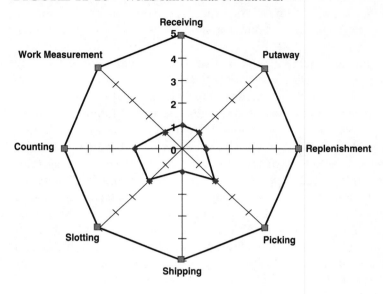

FIGURE 11-17   WMS technical evaluation.

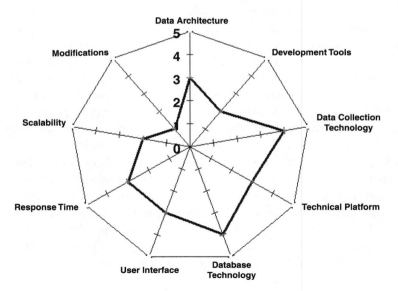

support your pursuit of world-class warehousing? I hope not. If the system will only support stage 1, no-class processes, you can expect similar processes and performance in your warehouse—no matter how great the technology is.

Just like you can't judge a book by its cover; you can't judge software by its interface (or marketing literature). Nearly every WMS vendor offers GUI interfaces, object-oriented designs, full-featured functionality, a grade-A client listing, and so on. To choose the right system and supplier you must "get under the hood to inspect the engine." You must meet the system designers. You must talk with the dissatisfied as well as the satisfied clients. You must learn about the origin of the system. (Many warehousing systems evolved from applications very far removed from warehousing, including accounting, customer service, general ledger, inventory management, and/or manufacturing.) You must meet with the engineers and analysts who will be assigned to your project. (For most WMS vendors, there are few highly qualified engineers and analysts. Those few are typically assigned to the largest and most prestigious accounts. If you are not included in that list, you may not be satisfied with the capabilities of the engineers and analysts assigned to your project.)

Another key decision in selecting a WMS vendor is whether or not to work with a provider of integrated solutions. Those providers typically provide a full suite of business applications, including customer service, purchasing, inventory management, general ledger, accounting, manufacturing management, and warehousing. Unfortunately, warehousing is typically an afterthought application for these providers, and the full-suite providers typically have very little expertise in warehousing. Instead, I strongly recommend an approach that incorporates world-class warehouse management functionality. If you are serious about achieving world-class warehousing, there is no other option. As an alternative to the integrated solution approach, We typically recommend the best-of-breed solution approach illustrated in Figure 11-18. This client-server web-enabled logistics solution was developed for a large textiles company. The centerpiece is a relational and object-oriented logistics database. The database is designed around logistics objects and is continuously updated in real-time. Information on customers, items, orders, carriers, shipments, and manufacturing schedules is included in the database. Attached to the database are best-of-breed systems for customer response, inventory, manufacturing, warehousing, and transportation. It is impossible to achieve world-class logistics without world-class logistics systems.

FIGURE 11-18   Logistics information system architecture.

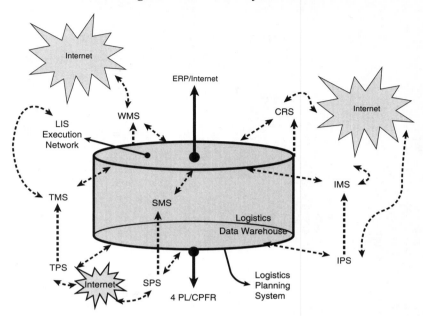

WMS Justification

I was recently invited by a large heavy machinery company to conduct a seminar on bar coding. Unfortunately, I know very little about bar coding. I explained that to the client and asked curiously if the real topic was bar coding or the benefits of bar coding. Immediately the client explained that they wanted to learn about the benefits of bar coding, including improved productivity, shipping and inventory accuracy, response time, and storage density. I was then able to explain that I knew a lot about how to make those improvements and that bar coding might or might not be on the road to those improvements.

We recently designed a WMS impact analysis for a client to help them focus on the fundamental benefits of computerizing warehouse operations. The WMS impact analysis chart (see Table 11-2) has a column for each WKPI and a row for each pactice that could not be achieved without the new system. If the practice could be achieved with alternative means, it cannot be included on the chart. The impact, positive or negative, in word, numbers, and direction of each new practice is recorded in the cells of the matrix.

TABLE 11-2 WMS Impact Analysis Chart

Activity	Current Practice	WMS Practice	Productivity Impact	Storage Density Impact	Accuracy Impact	Response Time Impact
INBOUND						
1. Unload & Stage	Manual, paper-based. CBLT with lift truck push-pull attachment. Place unit loads on pallets for putaway.	Major change is license plate scanning. Lot mixing on a storage pallet should not be permitted today.	⇔ Elimination of paperwork should offset additional scanning. Additional sorting of mixed SKU/code date pallets is good discipline and should be done today.	⇓ No more mixed SKUs on a pallet. Need 1/4 and 1/2 pallet openings to minimize the impact. Need additional area for pallet decomposition.		
2. Check, Match, Tag	Manual, paper-based. Paperwork prepared and receipts prelocated.	Real-time, paperless. Eliminates manual checking, matching, and tagging. All key entry eliminated.	⇑ 1 + office worker per DC. Won't send putaway operator to occupied location.		⇑ All key entry eliminated.	⇑ Takes 20 to 30 minutes out of the process per trailer.
3. Putaway	NAV transport to drop location and/or putaway. Paper-directed.	RF-directed. Extra scanning.	⇑ Less likely to send operators to occupied locations. Elimination of paper should offset additional scanning.		Location verification required.	
4. Interleaving	Not permitted.	Permitted via real-time communication and real-time redirection of operators.	⇑ Empty travel time is significantly reduced.			Empty travel time is significantly reduced.

224

5. Cross-docking	Not permitted.	Permitted via real-time directions to stage at shipping docks.	⇑ Critical capability for backorders. FIFO requirements limit opportunities.		
OUTBOUND					
1. Pallet-to-Door	Paper-directed NAV retrieval and drop. Checker verifies SKU, lot, quantity, and applies move tag. Transporter moves pallet to shipping dock.	RF-directed NAV retrieval and transport to shipping dock or drop zone.	⇑ Increased single handling. Checking step eliminated. Real-time operator redirection.	⇑ Pick location verification. Location is available as soon as location is emptied.	⇑ Pick location verification.
2. Replenishment to Bulk Picking Line	Paper-directed NAV drops pallet. Day's pick quantity transferred to empty pallet. Remainder returned to home location. Checker verifies SKU, lot, quantity, and applies move label.	RF-directed retrieval and move to dedicated position on case picking line.	⇑ Eliminates case picking to partial pallet. Eliminates putaway for remainder pallet. Eliminates bringing empty pallet to drop location.	⇑ Elimination of remainder pallet that previously occupied full storage location.	⇑ Pick confirmation.

TABLE 11-2 WMS Impact Analysis Chart *(continued)*

Activity	Current Practice	WMS Practice	Productivity Impact	Storage Density Impact	Accuracy Impact	Response Time Impact
3. Partial Pallet Picking	Paper-directed, pick-to-pallet jack. No pallet jack. No pallet build sequencing.	RF-directed. Transactions sequenced heavy to light to coincide with pick line layout.	⇑ Sequenced transactions should increase productivity. Key will be to maintain handsfree picking.		⇑ Improved via location confirmation.	
4. Checking	Manual check of outbound loads for load sequence and pick quantity.	Pick quantity verified at picking. Load sequenced verified on move.	⇑ Manual, checking function virtually eliminated.			⇑ Manual, checking function virtually eliminated.
5. Loading	Manual loading via CBLT.	Manual loading via CBLT.	⇔			
OVERALL			⇑ • Should permit a 10% to 20% productivity improvement per RDC. • If the planned training program is properly implemented, the learning curve should be no more than 3 months.	⇔ • Single SKU/ code date per LP should increase space requirements. However, this pracctice should be followed today. 1/4 and 1/2 pallet openings should minimize the impact. • Shallow racking for returns storage should improve density. • Real-time directed putaway will improve effective location utilization.	⇑ • Putaway and pick location verification will improve picking and inventory accuracy.	⇑ • Elimination of manual inbound checking, matching, and tagging.

The quantified, summarized, and annualized benefits of the new system are recorded in the last row of the chart. From the estimated annual benefits and the corporate payback period requirement, the justifiable system investment is derived. From that point on, the project must be managed to that budget.

WMS Implementation

Less than half of all warehouse management systems yield the performance and practice improvements promised during the justification phase. A major reason is that in many cases, the implementation process is flawed. One flawed approach is the big bang approach in which an operation tries to leap in one-step from a highly manual operation to a fully automated and integrated solution. There are several major problems with this approach. First, it takes so long that many of the problems the system was originally designed to address will have disappeared when it is time to implement. Second, many of the people involved in the selection and justification process will not be around to be involved in the implementation. Third, many of the benefits required to pay for the system occur after most of the investment has been made. Also, many of the benefits used to justify the system might be available for a much lower investment and in much less time than the big bang approach.

In a recent project (see Figure 11-19), we incrementally justified and implemented a full logistics information system. We began with the design of an object-oriented, relational logistics database and a definition of the ideal, fully integrated logistics information system. Once the database was populated, we attached PC-based profiling and decision support systems for warehousing (voice headset system), customer response, forecasting, inventory planning, and manufacturing. Based on the logistics gap analysis performed to justify the project, 50 percent of the projected benefits accrued from the first phase of the project. The first phase required only 10 percent of the projected investment requirements. In the second phase, the next logical system integration steps were taken as the PC-based warehousing and customer response systems were integrated into one client-server application and the forecasting, inventory planning, and manufacturing applications were integrated into another client-server application. These two applications were linked through real-time updates to/from an object-relational logistics database. This phase brought another 30 percent of the projected benefits for another 30 percent of the anticipated investment. As a result, less than one year into the project, 80 percent of the projected benefits had been realized for less than 40 percent of the anticipated investment. No further integration was justifiable on an incremental basis.

FIGURE 11-19   Logistics information systems evolution plan.

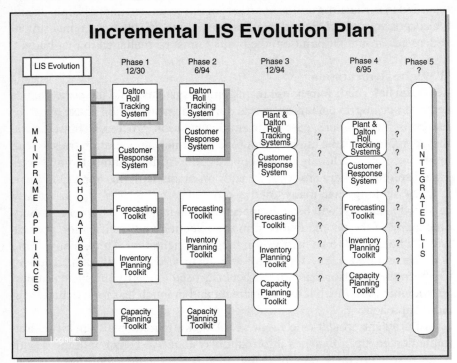

Another flaw in the big-bang approach is that the associated reengineering is typically done in series. Processes are redesigned, supporting systems are designed and implemented, and people are trained. Unfortunately, it is not until people begin to implement the new processes that the project benefits are realized. Instead, the processes should be redesigned, the supporting systems designed and implemented, and the people trained in parallel. We recently developed a reengineering process called *ConsulCation* to train the members of a cross-functional team as they work to redesign their warehousing and logistics processes. Simultaneously, the LIS infrastructure and PC-based profiling and decision support tools are being developed. This infrastructure and the PC-based tools serve as the springboard for more robust and integrated systems.

You may be familiar with the proverb that says when we are faithful with the little things, then we can handle the big things. That proverb also holds with logistics projects. Under the pressures of short term financial performance and increasing competition, we may yield to the instinct to bite off more than we can individually or corporately chew with respect to financial and/or human resources. To assist our clients with an incremental justification approach, we typically perform an incremental economic analysis of a proposed project. Figure 11-20 illustrates an example analysis.

In the figure, the initial project under consideration required a capital investment of $1,000,000 with a potential annual savings of $1,000,000. The payback on the project would be 1.0 years, strong enough to be funded in most U.S. organizations. However, a more detailed analysis of the initial proposal typically reveals a less expensive option that may yield a majority of the savings associated with the initial proposal. The reason is that the initial project proposal is typically derived from an automation plan proposed by a vendor, consultant, or an internal resource excited by a recent conference, magazine article, or vendor presentation. It is easy to justify automation for a poorly conceived process. It is almost impossible to be successful with automation in a poorly conceived process.

In incremental justification, we consider every possible alternative that could improve the current process. That discipline usually reveals a small capital investment combined with a variety of simplification techniques that can yield a dramatic improvement for a fraction of the investment and risk. In the example, a $200,000 investment was found to yield $800,000 in annual savings. The payback period on the low-risk proposal is 0.25 years or 3 months. This proposal should almost certainly be pursued because the risk

FIGURE 11-20   Incremental project justification approach.

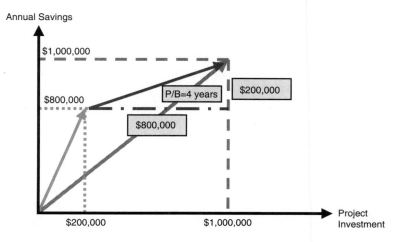

is low, the payback is high, and the underlying process should be simplified before any automation is deployed. In addition, by exposing the second option, the true economics of the initial proposal are revealed. That is, for an incremental investment of $800,000, an annual savings of $200,000 is available. The payback on this incremental proposal is 4.0 years, exposing the reality that a majority of the initial proposal was related to infrastructure that may or may not be required.

C H A P T E R

12

WAREHOUSE WORKFORCE DESIGN AND DEVELOPMENT

THE PLIGHT OF THE WAREHOUSE manager is not much better and perhaps worse than the plight of the transportation manager. Required to execute more transactions, in less time, with more items, with less margin for error, and with less skilled labor, the warehouse manager's role has risen to mission-critical. The capabilities of the warehouse workforce have also risen to mission-critical status. Unfortunately, the development and capabilities of most warehouse workforces and supporting information systems are lacking in the face of e-commerce, same-hour delivery, and no-fault performance. We recommend the following practices as supporting initiatives in what should be a strategic and ongoing program of warehouse workforce development.

12.1 SAFETY AND ERGONOMIC TRAINING
One reason the turnover of warehouse personnel is so high is due to a basic tenant of human psychology. When people feel threatened or unsafe in any environment, their natural reaction is to flee. If the dock is unsafe, if order pickers sustain back injuries, or if the workforce is infiltrated by drug users and/or pilferers, the instinct of the most qualified workers will be to flee. My experience with our clients is that the ones with the most stable

and productive warehouse working teams are the ones with the most developed programs for safety training, ergonomics, drug- and substance-abuse screening, and housekeeping.

12.2   TIME STANDARDS, INCENTIVES, AND PERSONNEL SCHEDULING

With warehouse worker availability at a premium and time of the essence, the ability to monitor, motivate, and schedule each task within the warehouse is a critical capability in warehouse workforce management. Time standards enable warehouse managers to develop staffing requirements in each area within the warehouse. Incentives for productivity and quality help to motivate excellent performance and reward outstanding work. Personnel scheduling minimizes the likelihood of bottlenecking in the warehouse and facilitates the movement of personnel between activities within the warehouse.

12.3   OPTIMAL MANAGEMENT-OPERATOR RATIOS

There was a move a few years ago toward self-directed work teams in warehouse operations. As warehouse activities have become more complex, as the availability of qualified warehousing professionals has declined, and as the fallacies of self-direction without adequate training and tools have been exposed, a renewed interest has arisen in the fundamentals of warehouse workforce management. One of the most important fundamentals of warehouse management is the span of control within the operations. Our experience shows that operator-supervisor ratios in excess of 17 to 18 do not permit adequate supervision and that ratios less than 13 to 14 are too costly.

12.4   CROSS-TRAINING

Cross-training is the practice of preparing warehouse operators to work in multiple areas within the warehouse. The practice is especially effective when the timing of activity peaks does not coincide in the operating areas in the warehouse. In those scenarios, cross-trained workers can move between the peak activity areas as workload mandates. Cross-training can reduce the overall staffing requirements in proportion to the ratio of the peak to average activity levels.

12.5   SOKO CIRCLES

Quality circles are nothing new. The concept originated in Japanese automobile factories where groups of workers would meet in small teams to coordinate problem-solving for quality issues on the production floor. Over ten years ago I borrowed the Japanese word for warehouse, soko, to coin the phrase *Soko Circles*. Soko Circles are quality circles working in warehouse operations. I have only seen the concept applied in a few warehouse operations in the United States. One of those is the JC Penney catalog distribution centers where problem-solving teams meet regularly to resolve quality issues on the warehouse floor. Another example is the Walt Disney World attractions merchandise DC where workers meet in continuous improvement teams to develop floor-level implementation plans for new warehousing initiatives. In both instances, the concept is the foundation for the management philosophy and works to foster excellent relationships between the warehouse management and the warehouse workforce.

At a time when warehouse quality and accuracy have become competitive differentiators, it is time for the warehouse workforce to become more prepared for and more involved in warehouse solution design and implementation. We worked recently with a large retailer in the design of a range of new warehousing initiatives. Part of the implementation plan was a series of training sessions for the entire warehouse workforce that shared the warehousing principles underpinning the new initiatives. The workforce could then understand the motivation for the new systems and procedures, and they embraced the new operating concepts based on their understanding as opposed to their directives.

12.6   1/2 × 2 × 3

There is an organizational philosophy that theorizes if you take the top 1/2 of the workforce and pay each of them twice as much, then you accomplish three times as much work as was previously being accomplished. I'm not sure where the theory came from, but I do believe the underlying principle has some merit. Our clients who focus rewards and attention on the top performers, who pay higher than the industry norms for qualified warehouse personnel, and who work to weed out the operators who are impeding the overall effectiveness of the entire workforce have much lower overall operating costs and much higher shipping accuracy.

Index

About the Author

EDWARD **FRAZELLE, PH.D.,** is president and CEO of Logistics Resources International, founder of The Logistics Institute at Georgia Institute of Technology, and director of the school's Logistic Management Series. As the former president of the International Material Management Society and a pioneer in today's logistics movement, Dr. Frazelle has trained more than 50,000 logistics professionals and helped more than 100 corporations and government agencies in the United States, Asia, Europe, and Latin America pursue and achieve logistics excellence. He has written or co-authored seven books, including Supply Chain Strategy, and numerous articles on logistics. His Website **www.LRILogistics.com** is recognized as one of today's most comprehensive and valuable resources for logistics information and instructional materials.